Rescued

Hope for Wounded Hearts

*The L*ORD *is close to the broken hearted and saves those who are crushed in spirit.*
(Psalm 34:18)

Only God can truly heal brokenness, rescue a wounded heart, and lovingly put the pieces back together again. He restores wholeness and breathes life into a stone-cold, deadened heart, unveiling His own heart and love in the process and bringing unexpected joy!

Rescued

Hope for Wounded Hearts

By Denise Gater

Unless otherwise indicated, all Scripture quotations are from
THE HOLY BIBLE, NEW INTERNATIONAL VERSION®, NIV®
Copyright © 1973, 1978, 1984, 2011 by Biblica, Inc.®
Used by permission. All rights reserved worldwide.

Scripture quotations marked (ESV) are from The Holy Bible, English Standard Version, copyright © 2001 by Crossway Bibles, a division of Good News Publishers.

Scripture quotations marked (NLT) are from The Holy Bible, New Living Translation, copyright © 1996, 2004, 2015 by Tyndale House Foundation.

Used by permission. All rights reserved.

For the sake of clarity, I have taken the liberty to capitalize all words in quoted Scripture references when they refer to deity.

About the Author

Denise Gater grew up in a loving family with devoted parents, being the middle of 5 children. They provided tremendous opportunity to excel in sports and education. Despite all this, Denise was in an extremely dark place emotionally by the age of 15. Severe knee pain cut short her competitive diving career, sexual abuse by her coach had been going on for years, and the weight of shame she hid left her numb, withdrawn, and hardened.

Although Denise's parents were loving, they had no belief in God. Surprisingly, it was her atheist father who encouraged her to go to a Young Life Camp that summer. It was there that her perspective completely changed about God and sparked hope and a desire to know Jesus intimately as her Savior and Lord.

Shortly after camp, her knee pain miraculously disappeared (coincidence after 18 months off? I think NOT) and she returned to diving, competing at an elite level, earning a gold medal at the Pan American Games. BUT most importantly, 30 years later, God brought His deeper inner healing to her wounded heart in a profound way. He entered the mess of her traumatic memories, from dark wounds long ago, and changed everything. He gave her a series of visions, beautiful images in her head that completely transformed her heart—a gift beyond words. Denise has shared her story and paintings in small groups, at women's retreats, in a Bible college classroom, at a creative arts gathering, and one-on-one whenever opportunity arises. It is a true story of hope and healing for those who have been wounded.

Denise received her BS in physical education from the University of Texas and her MS in exercise and sport sciences from the University of Arizona. She entered her career first as the assistant strength coach at the University of Arizona, then continued as an exercise physiologist and personal trainer at Canyon Ranch Resort and Spa in Tucson, Arizona. She was the age group diving coach for the Tucson Diving Club at the University of Arizona for eight years in addition to her full-time job. Her athletic endeavors were primarily in diving, however, she also enjoyed competing in Olympic-style weightlifting, finishing second in both the Clean & Jerk and the Snatch at the U.S. Weightlifting Federation Nationals.

She met her husband, David, during graduate school. They have been married over 30 years and have two wonderful daughters. Denise and David now live in Florida, where David serves as Chair of Physical Medicine and Rehabilitation at the University of Miami Miller School of Medicine. They have served as volunteers together in the ministry of Young Life for many years. Denise is now mentoring at the Glory House of Miami, who is "devoted to healing and restoring the lives of those who have suffered the abuse and exploitation of human trafficking" (www.gloryhouseofmiami.org). Any profits from this book will go directly to help this cause.

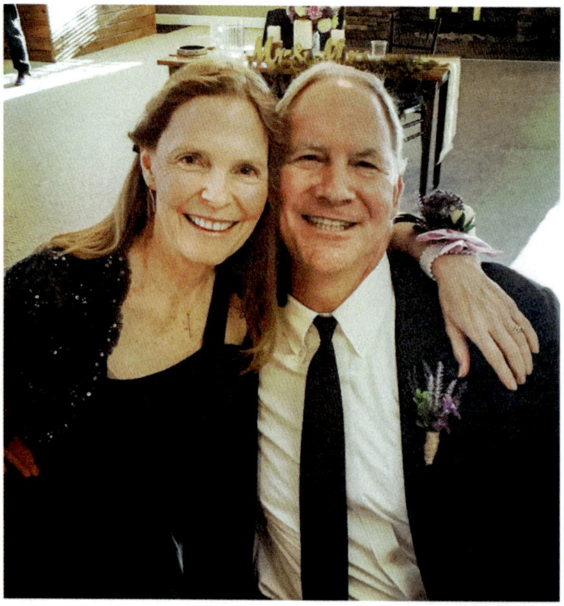

Dedication

I lay this book and these paintings on the altar before my Lord—Jesus. He has given to me a gift beyond words, and now I give it back to Him. I pray He will have His way with my offering. I am honored and grateful that He chose me to share through my life this incredible story of His redeeming love. I pray that my attempt to explain and illustrate His gift to me will not only offer hope, but also be a catalyst to deep inner healing and transformation in the hearts of others who have been wounded.

To my husband, David, who has poured himself out for me selflessly in so many ways throughout our relationship and has loved me with the unconditional love of Jesus. He stood by me through the good, the bad, and the ugly. He fought for my heart when I needed him most by praying boldly against the demons who sought to take hold…and they fled! He also helped me recognize and retrain my thought life by gently pointing out lies in my thinking and telling me the truth…over and over for many years. I could not have faced the memories that tormented me, laid myself bare, and processed what happened in counseling without him. He is my best friend, who carried me to the feet of Jesus for healing when I was paralyzed with wounds from my past. I admire, trust, and respect him immensely. He is such a gift to me from the Lord. He is truly the love of my life here on earth.

Table of Contents

About the Author — 5
Dedication — 7
Foreword — 11
Introduction — 13
About Visions — 16
Sharing My Experience — 17
Life Event Timeline — 18
Chapter 1: *Amy's Hug* — 20
Chapter 2: *The Journey* — 24
Chapter 3: *The First Rescue* — 28
Chapter 4: *The Box* — 34
Chapter 5: *The Reunion* — 40
Chapter 6: *Diving Out of the Box* — 44
Chapter 7: *Breath of Life* — 48
Chapter 8: *The Lie* — 54
Chapter 9: *Holy Shower* — 60
Chapter 10: *My Beloved* — 64
Chapter 11: *Wholehearted* — 68
Chapter 12: *A Transformed Heart* — 72
Chapter 13: *Leaning In* — 78
Chapter 14: *His Golden Girl* — 84
Chapter 15: *My Greatest Rescue* — 90
Acknowledgments — 97
References — 100

Foreword

History repeats itself.

Her story reveals His story.

I came to know Christ through Denise; I came to know Denise through Christ.

When I first met Denise, Christ revealed her to me in her true glory—beautiful, confident, rare in all the world, and lovable beyond belief—as He created her to be and as He perceived her to be, not only physically, intellectually, and emotionally, but also spiritually. I have been incredibly blessed.

Living in the shadowlands—the world as we know it—and subject to the lies of the enemy, however, had left her blinded, numb, ashamed, and completely unaware of her glory self. God brought her into my life to reveal my life and its purpose. And in the process, we've both grown closer to Him and closer to who He created us to be. I have been incredibly blessed!

Her story isn't for the weak of heart, nor for those who like fairy tale endings. It is raw, painful, fearful and heartrending. But it reveals her purpose. And His. Her story will remind you of yourself and who He created you to be. It is a story of tragic wounding and remarkable healing. The images captured by her heart will awaken your deepest emotions. And greatest hopes. Abundant life.

Her story reveals His story. And yours.

Be incredibly blessed!

David Gater, M.D., Ph.D.
Chair of Physical Medicine and Rehabilitation
University of Miami, Miller School of Medicine
and the Author's Incredibly Blessed Husband

Introduction

A Solemn Affirmation of Triumph
"They triumphed over him [Satan] by the blood of the Lamb and by the word of their testimony..."
(Revelation 12:11).

Testimony *"A solemn declaration or affirmation made for the purpose of establishing or proving some fact."*
(Webster's 1828 Dictionary)

When I was 45 years old, traumatic memories from my childhood began flooding my mind…as real and fresh as if the events causing them had just happened. Emotions erupted as I tried to stuff the memories back into the box I had locked them so carefully away in. For some reason, I couldn't. For years, these memories had been buried but not forgotten, yet now they were too strong for me to control. Under the weight of shame, I curled up in a ball on the couch and began weeping as the dark memories tormented me. At four o'clock in the morning, my husband David found me still on the couch that was now drenched with my tears. He tried to gently comfort me…but his touch made my skin crawl. He began to pray and finally was able to hold me as I cried in his arms and told him what was happening. He knew about my past early in our relationship—the sexual abuse from the age of nine to nearly 15—so thankfully, it wasn't a huge shock to him when the memories hit. However, in our twenty years of marriage, those memories had never been unleashed against me like this.

David and I had met in graduate school. I was six years into my eight-year battle with an eating disorder. For some reason, the Lord gave me a trust in David. I could be honest and completely myself with him. This gift of trust was supernatural because I did not trust men. I usually hid the "dark side" of my past from others, but David was different. He genuinely cared about me without wanting anything in return, and he was an excellent listener. We became close friends. I shared things with him early in our friendship that I had never shared with anyone, including all of the pain, shame, and anger from my past. He was patient, persistent, and gently pointed out lies in my thinking, sharing the truth with me in a sensitive way. He walked alongside me and loved me tenderly through my emotional roller coaster, way before we began dating.

God has given David wisdom and insight as to how to support and love me, knowing just what to do and when to do it. So two emotionally distraught days after he had found me on the couch at 4 a.m., he said it was time to find a counselor together. I knew he was right. I called my friend Nancy to see when we could get together. It was helpful that she was our pastor's wife. I knew she and her husband would be able to refer us to the right person. Now David and I were back on that emotional roller coaster, but it had grown considerably larger and more terrifying since I'd last been on it.

I chuckle now as I reflect on how much David loves riding real roller coasters. Thinking back to 1997, after he had finally completed his residency training in physical medicine and rehabilitation, he chose to celebrate by going to California's Great America to ride roller coasters with our 10-year-old nephew, Tyler. Tyler was the perfect choice of a companion since most of David's family and friends can't begin to keep up with him at an amusement park. I can still picture the two of them seated in the front of the roller coaster with arms held high and absolute glee shining from their faces—but I knew riding my roller coaster wouldn't be like that. Ready or not…the ride was already rushing forward with no slowing down in sight and no way to get off.

Nancy and I met together the very week I called her. Not only did she and her husband recommend an experienced counselor, but she prayed for me as well. She lifted me up to the Lord in prayer, seeing me as whole, perfect, and beautiful. She prayed that Jesus would soften my heart, which had been hardened by all my past wounds, and bring about His healing.

The psychologist recommended had been in marriage and family counseling practice for thirty years, with the last fifteen years specializing in trauma. On the way to our first appointment, tears streamed down my cheeks as feelings of fear and dread welled up with the knowledge that talking about my past would make it "real" again. I had spent countless years burying that hated part of my life, yet here it was—alive and assaulting me once again, making life unbearable. Having David by my side gave me courage and let me feel protected and loved, even though everything in me wanted to run. A picture of my small prayer team entered my mind. They were carrying me to the feet of Jesus for healing. This image calmed my heart and filled me with strength and hope.

After telling the counselor my story, he said there was good news and bad news. The good news was that my chances of recovery were very high. The bad news was that there was no quick fix technique to stop the sensation of my skin crawling, a sensation that accompanied the recurrence of my memories. Recovery was typically a long, slow, and painful process. It would require going back into the memory that had been tormenting me, experiencing it again, and in that wounded place…crying out to Jesus for healing. Then all I could do was wait to see what He would do.

NOOOOO! Reliving these memories was the last thing in the world I wanted to do! However, I couldn't live with their tormenting me like this either. I had known that someday I might have to face my past. As scary as it was…it was time.

David went to all the counseling sessions with me and was there to help me process what was happening after each one, which was an invaluable gift. We walked together every step of the way through this healing journey. The counselor also said to pray for the little wounded girl inside me.

A close friend prayed a special prayer for me early in this process. At the time, I felt overwhelmed with shame from the dark memories. She asked God to "take the lid off" this area of my life. As she prayed, I saw a big gift box from God. As He opened it, hope and anticipation filled my heart. It seemed like He was going to do something specific or give me something special in this area of my life. I wanted to hang on to that picture.

Over the next three months, the Lord gave me a gift beyond words, a series of visions (which I refer to as "rescues") that connected to form the story of His redeeming love, which resulted in deep inner healing. I never could have imagined being rescued like this, but I know one thing for sure—I WILL NEVER BE THE SAME.

"The Spirit of the Sovereign LORD is on me, because the LORD has anointed me to proclaim good news to the poor. He has sent me to bind up the brokenhearted, to proclaim freedom for the captives and release from darkness for the prisoners, to proclaim the year of the LORD's favor and the day of vengeance of our God, to comfort all who mourn, and provide for those who grieve in Zion—to bestow on them a crown of beauty instead of ashes, the oil of joy instead of mourning, and a garment of praise instead of a spirit of despair. They will be called oaks of righteousness, a planting of the LORD for the display of His splendor" (Isaiah 61:1-3).

"For He has rescued us from the dominion of darkness and brought us into the kingdom of the Son He loves in whom we have redemption, the forgiveness of sins" (Colossians 1:13).

Why He Was Sent

A profound encounter
   With Jesus
  Changed everything
Giving me a heart
  More fully alive to Him
   Intimate

  - A broken heart
Deeply healed
Free from torment
   And shame

- Reliving four traumatic memories
  Of deep wounds
   From long ago

  - Transformed
  Miraculous
Beauty without boundaries
  Life giving

 - Bringing me
From the dominion of darkness
  Into the kingdom
   Of the Son He loves

 - Binding up my broken heart
Setting this captive free
  Comforting me as I mourned
Bringing beauty out of the ashes
  Of my past
Giving me a garment of praise
  Instead of a spirit of despair

- Displaying His splendor
  In all His glory

- Only God
  Can do this

 - It is why
  He was sent

About Visions

If you are apprehensive or skeptical about the idea of visions from the Lord, I don't blame you. If God had not chosen to speak to me through them while completely transforming my heart, I would be skeptical too! God has many ways He chooses to communicate with us. More commonly, He speaks through our time of prayer or reading the Bible (His Word), and sometimes it's simply through an impression or "nudge" He places deep in our hearts, leading us to take action or giving us a clearer understanding in some area of our lives. God is not limited in the way He chooses to speak to His children. He deals with each of His beloved children in a personal and unique way. Visions, though not as common, are another way He chooses to speak to us.

In the Bible when God would give someone a vision, it was usually for a brief moment or a limited time period. My experience was similar to these Bible encounters. The series of visions that the Lord gave me happened off and on during a three-month period, and they ended as soon as He had completed His inner healing work within me. I had never had visions from the Lord quite like these before, and I haven't received any since. In each case, the visions that I had were in accord with God's written Word. They strengthened my relationship with God and brought revelation, hope, and comfort, rather than causing confusion.

There are a number of visions described in the Bible. Perhaps the most notable is in the book of Revelation, written by John, one of the disciples. The book documents a series of visions Jesus gave to John about the end times. For example, Revelation 1:1-2 says, "The revelation from Jesus Christ, which God gave him to show his servants what must soon take place. He made

---

A vision is "something seen in a dream, trance, or ecstasy; especially: a supernatural appearance that conveys a revelation."
– Merriam-Webster Dictionary

---

it known by sending his angel to his servant John, who testifies to everything he saw—that is, the word of God and the testimony of Jesus Christ." The Bible says John SAW the word of God and the testimony of Jesus. Although my visions were certainly not equivalent to God's divine revelation of Scripture—and I didn't see an angel—what happened to me throughout these healing visions might have been similar to what John experienced.

What I've learned, and I hope what you will learn as you read this book, is that God is not bound by our preconceived notions of who He is or how He chooses to move on earth or in our hearts. "As the heavens are higher than the earth, so are My ways higher than your ways and My thoughts than your thoughts" (Isaiah 55:9).

My prayer is that in sharing my story with you, you will SEE the loving heart of Jesus in a new way. If He can reach into and heal a wounded heart as broken as mine was, then He is able to do the same for you. Courageously cry out to Jesus and welcome Him into your pain. He wants to heal every area of your brokenness.

"For God did not send His Son into the world to condemn the world, but in order that the world might be saved through Him" (John 3:17).

"Now to Him who is able to do immeasurably more than all we ask or imagine, according to His power that is at work within us, to Him be glory in the church and in Christ Jesus throughout all generations, for ever and ever! Amen" (Ephesians 3:20-21).

Sharing My Experience

After the series of visions and my profound encounter with Jesus was over, I felt free from shame—completely healed and whole inside. I had an urgent desire to paint the visions so I would remember them all in vivid detail. I never wanted to forget. I longed to share the beauty of the visions and my story of inner healing with other "wounded hearts" so they could receive His healing as well. One clear problem kept me from this: I had never taken a painting or drawing class. The truth was, I had never really had much interest in art. For a number of reasons, it is quite miraculous that this book is in your hands at all. "With God all things are possible" (Matthew 19:26).

There are five avenues through which I've chosen to share my experience with you:

1. Personal Thoughts
To help the reader connect and understand the story more easily, "Personal Thoughts" were included at the beginning of each chapter. These sections are intended to give the reader a glimpse into my processing of these supernatural visions and the navigation of my feelings and thoughts during this time.

2. Visions
When a vision entered my mind, it was like having a dream while I was awake. Sometimes it seemed like I was watching a movie of myself (or a younger part of myself). However, most often I was a part of the interactive imagery.

3. Painting
There came a point where I felt like God wanted ME to paint the visions, so I signed up for a painting class. I must say that none of the paintings look exactly like what I saw and experienced in the visions. However, my painting improved over the years, and thus the paintings became more accurate over time. What you hold in your hands is the result of an eight-year process. Painting the visions became further therapy for me. My heart absorbed the healing more fully as I painted the visions. The very act of painting helped to ingrain all that I had learned and experienced through the visions.

4. Poetry
Immediately after the inner healing was over, I compiled my journal entries into a book. However, the words felt so incomplete without the visions. During the years of painting, I pondered and prayed that God would show me how to best share my story. Sharing what occurred in a poetic form to accompany the paintings finally felt right. My desire was to share from my heart and mind what had happened during each vision, as though I were experiencing it again.

5. Bible Verses (God's Word)
Sometimes during the vision or as I journaled about the vision experience later, particular Bible verses would come to mind. Also, as I read the Bible, occasionally a verse would jump off the page and immediately remind me of a vision I had experienced. I added these verses to my journal throughout the inner healing and even during my painting years. They affirmed that what I had experienced was in line with the Bible, and they became a part of my story.

LIFE EVENT Timeline

For a quick reference to some of the events written about in this book, I've included a short timeline and some of the corresponding healing visions – "Rescues."

Rescues

The timeline and order of the healing visions the Lord gave me:

FIRST RESCUE:
Age: 11
Sexual Abuse by Coach

SECOND RESCUE:
Age: 20
Eating Disorder, Double Life

THIRD RESCUE:
Age: 20
Motorcycle Accident

FOURTH RESCUE:
Age: 15:*
Home Break-In

*Note: The Fourth Rescue seems out of order, but this is how Jesus brought them up. He has His reasons. Jesus is not bound by time!

AGE

9 — Sexual Abuse from Age 9-14

1969 Family Christmas picture (Denise, bottom left, age 9).

My first diving meet at age 9.

13-14 — Two-time Age Group National and World Diving Champion

The U.S. team, 1973 World Age Group Championships, Belgium. (*Denise, (bottom right, age 13).*

Some notable teammates include: Jennifer Chandler, (top left) Olympic gold medalist in 1976. Bruce Kimball, (bottom, second from left) Olympic silver medalist in 1984, and Greg Louganis, (bottom, second from right) Olympic 4-time gold medalist – two in 1984 and two in 1988.

14 — Knee Pain

Knee pain from chondromalacia patellae forced me to quit diving. Treated with knee wraps, ice, and aspirin for 18 months! Began gaining weight.

15 — Home Break-In

First prayer to my sister's God (Jesus):
"Please don't let this man rape or kill my sister!"

AGE

15 — Young Life Camp

Second prayer at camp in Colorado:
"Jesus, if you are real, I want to know You! Show me that you are REAL!"

15 — God Healed My Knees

- God completely healed my knees! NO swelling or pain
- Began diving again

Practicing handstands on beam, age 15.

17 — American Cup Diving Champion

Accepted a full-ride diving scholarship to the University of Texas, 1977.

19-27 — Eating Disorder Began

My favorite dive! 1979 Senior Nationals (Austin, TX) placing second. Had just lost 20 lbs.

AGE

19 — Pan American Games Gold Medalist

1979 Pan American Games team at the Olympic Training Center. All of my teammates were Olympians. (Left-to-right: Coach Bryan Robbins, Phil Boggs, Barb Weinstein, Janet Ely, me, Greg Louganis and Coach Steve McFarland).

Denise wearing her gold medal from the Pan American Games (1979).

20 — AIAW National Diving Champion

Dual meet with the University of Arizona, my "home pool" before college.

20 — Motorcycle Accident

One month before Olympic trials, I had a terrible motorcycle accident, fracturing my L5 vertebra.

AGE

20 — Olympic Diving Trials 1980

- Trials for the Olympics to be held in Moscow
- Dove with a fractured vertebrae. Missed the cut for finals by less than one point
- Back surgery over Christmas: L5-S1 spinal fusion

21 — Malibu Young Life Camp

Since I couldn't dive, I served on summer staff as the lifeguard at Malibu YL Camp (Egmont, BC).

22 — Resumed Diving Competitions

- Final year of diving
- Team AIAW National Champions!
- I placed fifth

24 — Married David Gater

Love of my life, best friend and "lifting partner"!

32 — Hello, Brit!

- Our first precious daughter was born (1992 Tucson, AZ)
- David delivered her…well, I helped! (ha)

AGE

34 — Welcome, Felicia!

- Our second amazing daughter was born (1994 Sacramento, CA)
- David delivered her as well, but he had to perform some life-saving measures upon her arrival

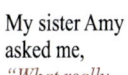

42 — Amy's Healing Hug

My sister Amy asked me, *"What really happened to you as a child?"* The Lord used this memory to begin healing my wounded heart two years later.

44 — Memories of Abuse Triggered

- Our daughters were now the age I had been during the sexual abuse.
- David and I started counseling. The Lord began entering my traumatic memories through visions, resulting in deep inner healing. I began journaling.

45-52 — Learning to Paint

Wanting to document the visions, I began taking painting classes, using soft chalk pastels.

CHAPTER ONE

Amy's Hug

"But the Counselor, the Holy Spirit, whom the Father will send in my name, He will teach you all things, and will remind you of all that I said to you" (John 14:26).

Personal Thoughts

As I entered into the first memory that had been tormenting me, complete desperation took over as I sought Jesus for healing. I couldn't find Him. It was awful! Just before I gave up, a verse came to mind that gave me a glimmer of hope: "'You will seek me and find me when you seek Me with all your heart. I will be found by you,' declares the Lord, 'and will bring you back from captivity'" (Jeremiah 29:13-14). Upon remembering this verse, I tried harder to find Him in this dark memory, but I wasn't able to.

Filled with the stress and emotion of reliving the dreaded memory, I needed to exercise, so I put on a worship CD and began walking uphill on the treadmill. It felt good to breathe hard and move to the music. I began to relax, and my head began to clear of the dark memory.

The words of one of the songs on the CD caught my attention, *"Suddenly I feel you holding me…."* These words prompted me to think about a question the counselor had asked me at our first appointment: "Have you ever pictured Jesus holding or hugging you?" As I talked with the Lord, His first vision came to me. It was not a vision from the dark memory that had been tormenting me but an image that opened the door to a life-changing encounter and journey with Jesus. His work of inner healing began slowly, with someone familiar, someone I dearly love.

"I'm So Sorry!"

Amy's Hug

"Have you ever pictured Jesus
    Holding or hugging you?"
The counselor asked.
    I hadn't.

– Picturing myself
The bleeding woman
    Who can't quite touch Jesus
    For healing

– Why can't I touch You?
Coming so close at times
    Then vanishing
    Always out of reach
    For me
    It seems

– A memory triggered
My sister, Amy, hugging me
    Her tears flowing
    Yet I felt
    Numb or dead inside
    A heart of stone
Unable to receive her hug

– She asked
"What really happened to you
    As a child?"

– I love Amy
    Bold
    Yet gentle

– Besides my husband
    No one
    Had ever asked
For DETAILS

– While sharing
    Details
Her tears began

– Revelation washed over me
    The wounded little girl
    Inside me
Needed that hug
    Those words

– The image changed
My adult form shrank down
    Becoming a girl in her arms

– This time
I heard her words
    "I'm SO SORRY
You had to go through all that!"
Her words pierced my soul
    Sinking deeply to my core

– I began
    Weeping…
    Grieving
I hadn't cried before
    Not like that
Floodgates unlocked and flew open
    For a long time

– Those words
I desperately needed to hear
    As a child
    But never did

– No one knew
    So alone…

– This time
    I heard her words
    Received her hug
    Felt her touch
In this young
    Wounded place
Where it held deep meaning

– I sensed the Lord
Holding me through Amy's hug
    That day

– My inner healing
From sexual abuse
    Had finally begun

CHAPTER TWO

The Journey

*"For I am the L*ORD *your God, who takes hold of your right hand and says to you, Do not fear; I will help you"* (Isaiah 41:13).

*"The Sovereign L*ORD *is my strength; He makes my feet like the feet of a deer, He enables me to go on the heights"* (Habakkuk 3:19).

Personal Thoughts

After experiencing "Amy's Hug" and the breakthrough of grieving, I decided to begin my next time on the treadmill by listening to the same CD and hope the Lord would do something more. I intended to go into the dark memory again. I prayed that the Lord would bind any distractions that would keep me from opening my ears to hear and the eyes of my heart to both see and understand all that He wanted to do. I prepared my heart and began worshipping Him with the music.

The same song caught my attention. It was a song I wasn't really familiar with, entitled "Sweep Me Away."[2] With the words "suddenly I feel your hand in mine," the next vision began. Again, what I was seeing wasn't the dark memory that had been tormenting me. Although the song was not well-known to me, the Lord used not only the words of this song but also something familiar and with deep meaning to me as I began this journey with Him.

"It was frightening, yet hopeful..."

The Journey

"Suddenly
I feel your hand
In mine"
The music played

- An image came to mind
Jesus reached to help me
I took His hand
We were climbing
UP
A steep, rocky mountain
A beautiful stream on my right

- He carried a young girl
A child
ME!
Carrying her
A long time

- Uncanny
This scene
Like a tapestry in my home
Coming to life[3]

- "Don't be afraid," Jesus said
Caught completely off guard
I held my breath
Hearing so clearly

- Words from the tapestry
"Be not afraid"

- "Okay", I responded
Out loud!

- This mountain imagery
Brought to mind a favorite book
Hinds Feet on High Places[4]
And the main character
Little Miss Much Afraid

- Suddenly
I saw her guides
Sorrow and Suffering
Coming down the mountain
FOR ME!

- **It was frightening!**
Yet hopeful…
My desire for healing grew
As I recalled
The end of the story

- Little Miss Much Afraid
Healed
Given a new name
Grace and Glory
Her guides' new names
Joy and Peace
I wanted that!

- A difficult journey had begun
To the High Places
Just like Much Afraid
Following and surrendering ALL
To the Good Shepherd
Jesus

- Following the path
He'd chosen for me
Steep
Treacherous climbing

- Total trust and surrender
Essential
Eyes fixed on Him
And Him alone

- Then it hit me…
For the first time
I was touching Jesus!

"*Even to your old age and gray hairs I am He, I am He who will sustain you, I have made you and I will carry you; I will sustain you and I will rescue you*"
(Isaiah 46:4).

CHAPTER THREE

The First Rescue

"He reached down from on high and took hold of me; He drew me out of deep waters. He rescued me from my powerful enemy, from my foes, who were too strong for me. They confronted me in the day of my disaster, but the Lord was my support. He brought me out into a spacious place; He rescued me because He delighted in me"
(Psalm 18:16-19).

Personal Thoughts

My aerobic exercise time seemed to be a natural place for me to seek the Lord, so I continued doing this about three to four days each week as I listened to the same CD. Since I was working part-time, I used my days off to seek the Lord in this way. I had been an athlete, strength coach, and personal trainer for many years and had a well-equipped gym in our home. My journey was an emotional one, so I appreciated the privacy of our little gym, where I could let loose and weep if needed. I could talk to the Lord out loud or even yell—all of which happened! I began my workouts walking on the treadmill. I felt like I was hiking on a journey with Jesus. After about twenty minutes on the treadmill, I would switch to a different machine (elliptical, stair machine, rowing, or bike). Aerobic exercise was mindless for me, so it allowed me to fill my thoughts with the Lord and pay attention to what He wanted me to do. The counselor had advised that forty-five minutes was as long as he wanted me to delve into any tormenting memory. Exercise and the CD helped me limit my time to his recommendation.

This time I began my workout in the same manner: preparing my heart and praying for the Lord to bind distraction, open my ears to hear, and open the eyes of my heart to see and understand all He wanted to reveal. As the song "Sweep Me Away" began to play, the imagery of "The Journey" with Jesus began again.

We were climbing up the mountain, and He was carrying the little, wounded girl —me as a child. The climbing was hard, and my anticipation grew as I wondered what would happen next. Then the imagery changed, and the dark memories of the sexual abuse by my coach took over. The last time I had gone into these memories, I couldn't find Jesus. Clearly, it was the Lord's timing to try again.

The poem "The First Rescue" begins with the memories as they were first triggered, followed by entering into the darkest, most hated memory. It was in this wounded place where I felt like a little girl again, crying out to Jesus in complete desperation.

"Rescue me this time!"

The First Rescue

A load too heavy to bear
A burden not intended
    But mine to carry
       Alone
Since childhood

- Suddenly,
    The dark memories
Torment me!
    Overtaking me
  Like powerful waves
    Shoving me underwater
      Suffocating
Disorienting

- Emotion erupts
    Dissociating
      Transporting me
    From present
To past

- **NO!**
This CAN'T be happening!

- These memories
    Were "under control"
    Deliberately stuffed
      Into a box
    Buried
In the deepest
    Darkest
      Part of my heart
Locked up
    Left for dead

- But not forgotten

- How did they escape?
Who let them out?
    They are alive again
Attacking me like demons
    Tormenting and dark
Evil and ugly
    Shameful
      So shameful

- The talons of these memories
    Sink deeper
Into my mind
They won't let go!
    Digging deeper each time
      Getting a stronger hold

- Taking me back
    To that
      Terrible place
    Trapped
Reliving the nightmare
    Over and over
      Unrelenting!

- Gentle touch
Makes my skin crawl
A wave of disgust
    Washes over me
Repelling in response

- I can't live like this!
Desperate for help

- Fear
    Seeps in
The battle
    Too great
The burden of shame
    Too heavy

- HELP ME, dear Jesus!
You are my only hope
    Omnipresent God
You were there
    I didn't know you then
Didn't cry out to you

- *Jehovah El Roi*
    The God who sees
You see what happens
    In secret
You saw it all

- You didn't rescue me then
    Yet here I am
    Back in that very place
      Reliving it

- Rescue me this time!
    Lord Jesus
Sweep me away
    In Your mercy!

The First Rescue – continued

–Where are you?
I know You are here
You said
If I seek You
With all my heart
I will find You

–I'M SEEKING YOU NOW
WITH EVERYTHING IN ME!

–**WHERE ARE YOU?**

–Quietly
You appear
And come close
I see You!

–Tears blur my vision
But I know it's You
Light radiating
In the darkness
Of the room

–You scoop me
Off the bed of pain and shame
Saying
"It's not your fault…
This is not what I intended"

–As we begin to leave
You stop

–Taking evil items
From the room
Then throwing them
Through the wall
Into a lake that appeared
Beyond the wall

–As they hit the surface
It becomes
A lake of fire!
Like lava
Burning them up
Taking my breath away

–Streams of tears
Flow unhindered
You are rescuing me!
Out of this
Hated room
Out of this
Tormenting memory

–You sweep me away…
Entering a mountain scene
Far away
Another world
So peaceful
So beautiful

–We are on a journey
Climbing UP
Breathing hard

–That horrible memory
Burned into my soul
Transformed forever
Into something beautiful
Now a memory
Of rescue and deliverance!

–Gratefulness
Floods my heart and soul!
Your mercy
Miraculous

–**Overwhelmed**
You came
For **ME!**

"You will seek Me and find Me when you seek Me with all
your heart, I will be found by you,' declares the Lord,
'and will bring you back from captivity'"
(Jeremiah 29:13-14).

"They will know that I am the Lord, when I break the bars of their yoke
and rescue them from the hands of those who enslaved them"
(Ezekiel 34:27).

CHAPTER FOUR

The Box

*"I will give you a new heart and put a new spirit in you;
I will remove from you your heart of stone and
give you a heart of flesh"*
(Ezekiel 36:26).

Personal Thoughts

Still in awe of "The First Rescue," I continued journaling everything that happened after "Amy's Hug" so I wouldn't forget what the Lord had done. I also wanted to share the details with the counselor on our next visit, which wouldn't take place for three weeks. I read my journal over and over in amazement. Each time I read, gratefulness and praise filled my heart. I never realized Jesus could heal or change memories like those that haunted me. This realization was huge for me. I knew Jesus lived outside of the limitations of time and that nothing was impossible for Him, but what Jesus was doing in my life was beyond even my wildest imagination!

The abuse occurred before I knew Jesus. As I was growing up, God was not a part of our household. I grew up in an atheist home, and we never went to church, although my mom and dad were good, moral, loving parents with a strong marriage. I didn't know how to deal with the abuse, so I stuffed it as deeply as I could inside my heart. It didn't even occur to me that I should tell my parents what was happening. Things like this were not talked about back then, and I was young and didn't understand it at all at first.

One day I began my workout as usual, and the first three songs on the CD helped me prepare my heart and bind distraction. I praised Jesus and prayed that He would open my ears to hear, that the eyes of my heart would see and understand, and that He would completely have His way with me. I did not want my imagination to take over in any way and prayed that God would not allow this to happen. I knew that healing must be led and guided by Him. This routine of praise and prayer as I began to exercise was followed by a time of journaling and reflection. At that moment, I noticed the song on the CD that was playing: "Prepare the Way."[5] The words of the song reminded me to prepare my heart for the Lord.

"Heal those broken, shattered places that need Your touch."

The Box

"Prepare the way
Prepare the way of the Lord"
The music played

- Suddenly, the imagery began
I was in a room
In my heart
Appearing like
A red rock cave
In Arizona

- But strangely
There was snow everywhere
I began shoveling snow –
Of course,
To prepare a way for the Lord!

- There was a dark, cold part
Off to the left
I became
A little girl again
Going back into the darkest
Shadowy part

- Somehow
I knew where I was going
And what was there!

- Taking hold
I brought it out –
My box
Of bad memories

- I opened the lid
Giving the box
To Jesus
Who had appeared

- Inside the box
Were rocks
Broken rocks
From my heart of stone

- Emotion flooded me
As revelation came
Never before realizing…

- No access had been given Him
No permission granted
Or prayer spoken
Regarding THAT part
Of my heart!

- I didn't know Him then…

- Determined to forget
Rejecting that hated part of myself
Wounded beyond repair
It all was stuffed as deeply as possible
Closed off
Buried and left for dead
Moving on the best I could in life
With the rest of my heart

- Then His light
Began to move
Into the darkest
Hidden areas
Of my cold heart –
Exposing it all

- I prayed…
Make my heart
FULLY ALIVE
To You, Lord!
Heal those broken
Shattered places
That need Your touch

The Box – continued

- The imagery changed
  A new scene
  In Heaven
  Before Jesus on His throne
  Holy
  Majestic
  Dressed in brilliant white

- I dropped to my knees
  Laying the box
  At His feet

- He lifted me
  Onto His lap!
  Like a Dad
  With His child

- It felt safe
  In His arms
  I nestled in
  Close to His heart

- He was very gentle
  Tender
  Towards me

- Suddenly
  A strong feeling stirred within
  I KNEW
  He was transforming
  The broken rocks
  Into something of great value…
  Priceless treasure!

- Streams of beautiful
  Multicolored light
  Radiated from the box

- Warmth
  Hope for healing
  And the future
  Filled my heart

"The lamp of the LORD searches the spirit of a man; it searches out his inmost being" (Proverbs 20:27).

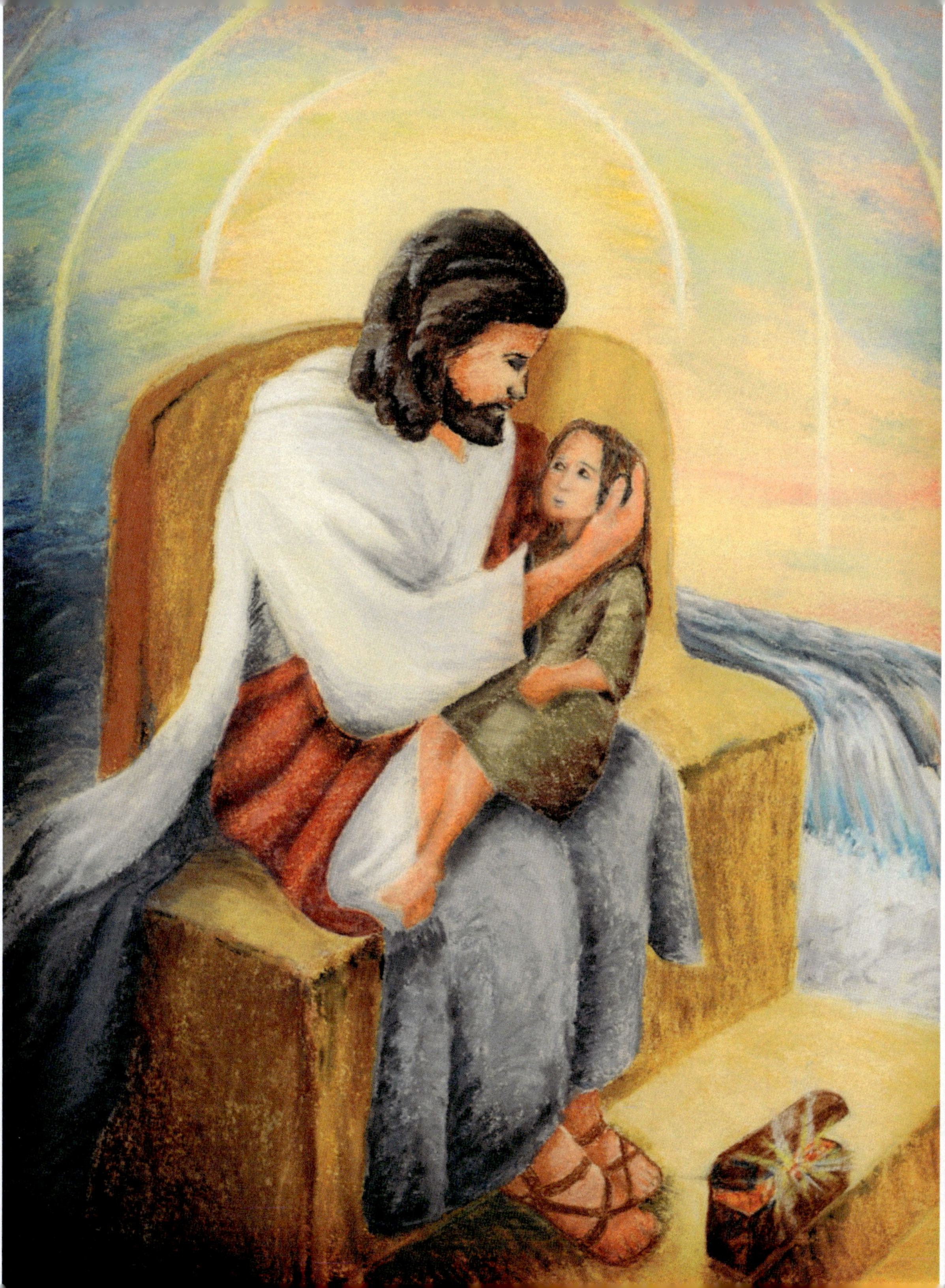

CHAPTER FIVE

The Reunion

"He has sent me to bind up the brokenhearted...."
(Isaiah 61:1).

Personal Thoughts

The visions surrounding both "The Journey" and "The Box" took place over a few separate days. Each vision would pick up where the last one left off, sometimes overlapping – like pushing rewind and replaying part of a movie over again before moving on to something new. At times, it was like watching a movie of myself (or a younger version of myself). Most often I was an interactive part of the imagery. My faith and anticipation grew with each new encounter. Something significant happened almost every time I got on the treadmill and pressed in to Jesus during this three-month period of inner healing.

I was completely drained after each session, making a long nap in the afternoon absolutely essential. The counselor had warned me of this potential effect and had told me to plan naps into my schedule, as well as to lower my expectations of productivity on those days. His advice was extremely helpful.

The day before this next vision, "The Reunion," fleeting glimpses of images and whispers flickered through my mind—even while I was driving to work. These scattered images were a new experience. I knew something big was coming….

"I'm sorry you were so alone."

The Reunion

Fleeting images
　　Whispers heard
　　　　During the day
Jesus saying
　　"You two
　　Need to get back together!"

　　- Something was coming
Anticipation grew

　　- Later
The full imagery began
　　Back in my heart room
In the red rock cave

　　- Jesus was there
With a little girl
　　Me as a child

- With me, as an adult, standing there
She was hesitant
　　Hiding behind Jesus' robes
　　　　Fearfully peeking out

　　- I had absolutely hated her
Rejecting that part of myself
　　Long ago

- Now with daughters of my own
　　I looked at her more closely
　　　　Compassion
　　　　　　Filled my heart

　　- "I'm sorry
　　I was so mean to you!"
There was such
　　Loneliness
　　Darkness
　　　　Fear and pain
　　　　　　In her

　　- "I'm sorry
You had to go through all that!
　　It wasn't your fault…
　　Will you forgive me?"
Knowing I had treated her ruthlessly
　　Rejected her harshly
　　Even blamed her

　　- Reaching for her
She came to me
　　I hugged her
Welcoming her back

　　- Intense weeping began
Feeling all she represented

　　- "I'm sorry you were
　　SO ALONE…"
　　　　No one to talk to
Heavy with shame

　　- Heal this little girl
I prayed silently
　　As we hugged

　　- Her hug back showed
She had forgiven me
　　I realized
She was part of me again

　　- Jesus stood close
His arms of protection around us

　　- Suddenly
He said with His eyes
　　"Let's go"
Back on the journey path
This time
Reaching a plateau
　　Not climbing UP anymore

- He carried
The little girl
　　As we walked
　　　　Side by side

- Looking over I saw
She was out cold
　　　　Asleep on His shoulder

- Like a hurt child
　　Cries and cries
Then suddenly
Falls fast asleep!

　　- Her face
　　　　So peaceful…

　　- I knew
She was SET FREE
　　　　That day

　　- His sweet peace
Washed over me

- Jesus whispered
"I love you"
　　And drew me close
"Really?"
　　"REALLY!"
And He kissed my head

CHAPTER SIX

Diving Out of the Box

*"I will restore to you the years
that the swarming locust has eaten"*
(Joel 2:25 ESV).

Personal Thoughts

After "The Reunion," I finally had my next counseling appointment. Since we had not met for three weeks, I had so much to share that I had to bring my journal just to keep track of it all. My counselor wrote frantically as I shared this first series of visions and my encounter with Jesus.

When I finished, he was stunned. He put his pad down and was utterly speechless. He looked over his notes, shaking his head, not speaking for several minutes. His complete astonishment validated what had happened almost as much as what he finally said in response. He called it a "textbook perfect model of inner healing, complete, with everything in the right order." He had never seen it go so quickly, not to mention that it had all taken place outside of his office. In his experience, the amount of progress made in these three to four weeks usually took closer to a full year. "When the Spirit moves, He MOVES!" he said, continuing to shake his head in wonder throughout our appointment. "I will praise the Lord, who counsels me…" (Psalm 16:7). All of the visions occurred at home, while I was alone, with the Holy Spirit leading the way. The counselor's response was extremely encouraging. He expected this model to become my "blueprint" for any more inner healing in the future.

I am so grateful for God's mercy of speed through the first part of this counseling process. As a diver and later an Olympic-style weightlifter, I have always preferred high intensity and short duration in most everything I do. God certainly knows that about me and let me dive in with full force.

The sweet peace I felt after the little girl was "set free" stayed with me. My skin stopped crawling, and I was no longer tormented by memories of the sexual abuse. When memories do enter my mind, the memory of Jesus rescuing me trumps them all and leaves me praising Him. The Enemy has lost his power over me in this area of my life.

I felt I was almost done with professional counseling, but I also felt the need to continue to pursue Jesus as I had been doing. This made the next vision very unexpected. Another broken part of me emerged disturbingly. At first I was shaken and enraged. Clearly, the Lord was not finished. I had only just begun my journey.

"He restored good memories."

Diving Out of the Box

The imagery began
With additional snow
In a different part of my heart
   I started shoveling

- When I saw her,
Anger flared
   Thinking I was
   DONE with her!

- Hating that part of me

- Horrible memories
Began flooding my mind
   Living a double life
   Enslaved to an eating disorder
   Eight agonizing years

- The bad memories
The sexual abuse
   The eating disorder
   The motorcycle accident
   Were so closely linked
   With diving
They drowned out
   All the good memories
And good side of me
   During college

- Impossible to separate
   Good from bad
All these memories
   Shoved deeply into the box

- Looking closer at her
I was overcome with surprise,
   Discovering she was
The "good side" of me
   Living a double life

- By giving Jesus access
To my box of bad memories,
He began to show me
There was more in there
   Than pain

- He began to restore
Good memories
The joys and highs of diving
   That pleased Him

- Performing
For an "Audience of One"
   Full body worship
For God Almighty
   Sitting on His throne
Watching me
   From an open portal
     In Heaven

- In His presence
   Full of joy
Sensing His pleasure

- Opening my box
He restored good memories
   Winning the Pan Am Games
   AIAW Nationals
   American Cup
Age Group World Championships

- Suddenly
I became the one in His arms
He threw me
   UP HIGH
Into the air!

- Instinct took over
   Diving
   Flipping
     Twisting
Landing back in His arms
   Then UP again for more!
Diving into the water
   Then finding myself
Back in His arms
   To FLY UP again

- A holy trampoline

- We were both having
   So much FUN!
   I heard Jesus
     Laughing with joy
Every trick different
   Every dive perfect

- Until then, the good memories
   Couldn't be separated
From the pain of the bad memories

- After this encounter,
For the first time in many years,
   Special pictures and awards
   Could be set out
To enjoy and remember
   As He intended

- Now able to look at them
   Remembering good memories
   Not just the pain

- A precious gift
Beauty and treasure
   Restored

CHAPTER SEVEN

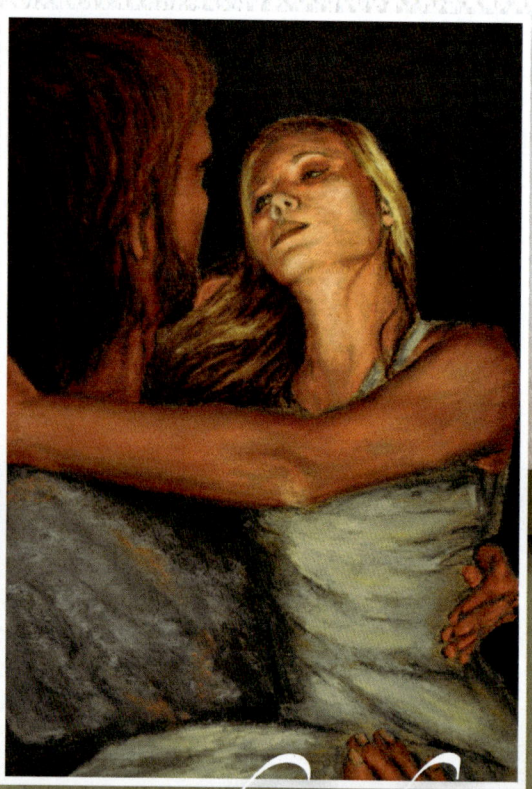

Breath of Life

"This is what the Sovereign LORD says to these bones: I will make breath enter you, and you will come to life"
(Ezekiel 37:5).

Personal Thoughts

That night I began to share with David how it seemed that God wasn't finished with my college self yet, even though I thought He had healed that part of me seventeen years before when the restricting, binging and purging had lifted. It was as though He was still working to redeem the ashes of my past and make them beautiful again. Yet I had been extremely angry and shaken when I first saw my college self again in the room of my heart. I was enraged that she and all her issues had invaded my present life.

In response to my discovery that God still had work to do on my college self, David made, what seemed to me, a flippant comment: "I'm not surprised." Instantly, I snapped into a fiery, irrational rage. My heart and mind hardened in defense. Lies that felt like truth at the time flooded my thoughts and fueled my fire. Verbal jousting ensued as we attacked each other's blindness. All of a sudden, it seemed that he had absolutely no idea what I was going through.

I felt utterly alone. Retreating, I withdrew into isolation, no longer wanting him to be a part of my recovery. He gave me time to cool down, but when he came to me, I was still as infuriated and hardened as before. Instead of talking or fighting, he began praying boldly against the demon that had taken hold of me, and I tangibly felt its presence lift off of me. It was startling how different I felt after it left. I could relax. I was instantly receptive and grateful for Dave's presence and for his understanding that there were dark forces at work, twisting my thoughts into destructive lies. He held me as I lay down. Exhaustion overtook me as I immediately drifted off into a deep sleep. David fought for my heart that night like a warrior in battle. He followed Paul's advice from Ephesians 6:10-12:

"Finally, be strong in the Lord and in His mighty power. Put on the full armor of God, so that you can take your stand against the devil's schemes. For our struggle is not against flesh and blood, but against the rulers, against the authorities, against the powers of this dark world and against the spiritual forces of evil in the heavenly realms."

Even still, I dreaded what was coming next, fearful of where God would take me and what I would find. During my next workout, the Lord confirmed my suspicions that He was going to unearth and restore this dark side of my college self.

"He began... breathing His breath of life into her."

Breath of Life

As the imagery began
   In my heart room
     A fresh layer of snow
       Appeared

-After shoveling a path
Preparing the way for Jesus
   I saw her
     Hiding in the darkness
       Always hiding

   -Sick and pale
Colorless
   Except
     Wild green eyes
       Frightening
         Demonic

-She was uncontrollable
   The "dark side"
     Of my double life
       In bondage
   To an eating disorder

   -I pulled her
     UP from the snow
And carried her
     To Jesus
       Who appeared

   -The scene changed
     As He swept her away
And carried her colorless form
   In His arms
UP the mountainous journey path
     To the top

-I followed
Watching from behind

-He began tenderly
Slowly
   Breathing into her
     His breath of life

   -As His breath
Touched her skin
     She turned
Sparkling gold
     Like a bright light
But more beautiful

-As His breath moved
From head to toes
     It transformed her
       Pale skin
Into a vibrant color

-He resurrected the life
     Drained out of her
During those eight years
     Of bondage

-It was stunning

   -Like Aslan
Bringing the stone creatures
   Back to life
In the White Witch's Castle[6]

   -Transforming her
Once pale and dead
   Now vibrant and alive
Color and life restored

-The scene changed again
The motorcycle accident
     Now out of the box
Of painful memories

-Slow motion
Flying through the air
   Sensing the Lord
Catching me
     Setting me down
       No pain

-Knowing
Without a doubt
As I lay in the street
   Full of broken glass
     He was there

-Jesus entered the memory
     Scooping me up
   Off the street
     Of glass

-Sweeping me away
     Taking me back
Into my heart room
     Holding me
       In His arms

-I remembered the pain
   The timing
Before Olympic Trials
     My life dream shattered
       Out of control

Breath of Life – continued

‒ Broken
Emotionally and physically
 Even standing up straight
  Shooting pain

‒ Diving in the
Olympic Trials anyway
 Despite a fractured vertebra

‒ Each press
  Of the diving board
Stabbing pain into my back
   Powerless to press hard
Unable to reach full height

‒ Completing the Trials
Missing finals
 By less than a point

‒ Back surgery
No diving
For months

‒ Competing
My last year
 But never the same

‒ This memory
 Such deep loss
Too painful to grieve back then

‒ Now full grieving unleashed
Like water bursting through a dam
Once restrained...now rushing forth

‒ God's perfect timing
Now able to receive His deep comfort
 Filling the empty places
  As only He can

‒ Now, years later
Knowing His ways
 Are higher than mine

‒ He brought eternal good
From this unexpected
   Traumatic event

‒ Looking back
  I see how
He changed my perspective
  The year of my recovery

‒ Serving on summer staff
  At Young Life Camp
Learning what was most important
   In life
   And to Him

‒ Recalling time with
One precious high school student
  At Young Life Camp

‒ Somehow I sensed
 Her depression
  Her pain
   Suicidal

‒ Discovering later
She had a plan and the means
  to take her life
There at camp

‒ Hours spent
 Talking at the pool

‒ Her life was changed
That week she met Jesus
 Filled with hope
And a desire to live
  To the FULL
   His way

‒ I realized
This young teenager's life
 Here and for eternity
Was far more important to God
Than my being an Olympian

‒ His ways
  His priorities
Higher than mine

‒ But now I had a glimpse
  Of His heart
He sees His children
  Their redemption
  More precious
Than their own temporary glory
  Or comfort

‒ A huge lesson
Learned

"'For My thoughts are not your thoughts, neither are your ways My ways,' declares the Lord. 'As the heavens are higher than the earth, so are My ways higher than your ways and My thoughts than your thoughts'" (Isaiah 55:8-9).

"And we know that in all things God works for the good of those who love Him, who have been called according to His purpose. For those God foreknew He also predestined to be conformed to the image of His Son, that He might be the firstborn among many brothers and sisters" (Romans 8:28-29).

"The thief comes only to steal and kill and destroy; I [Jesus] have come that they may have life, and have it to the full" (John 10:10).

CHAPTER EIGHT

The Lie

(Painted by my niece, Becky Knight Vermette)

*"Behold, You delight in truth in the inward being, and
You teach me wisdom in the secret heart"*

Personal Thoughts

It amazed me how tender and gentle Jesus was with my dark side, although I had loathed this uncontrollable girl for years. She nearly destroyed me. Honestly, though I despised her, I sometimes felt apathetic toward her, not caring that she might succeed. I started to realize there was more to her than just my sinful nature. There was also a demonic presence involved. An intense battle was raging for control over my heart and mind.

Jesus said in John 10:10, "The thief comes only to steal and kill and destroy. I came that they may have life and have it abundantly (ESV)." After listening to Christian psychologists Judith MacNutt and John Eldredge, I started to understand that the Enemy seeks out opportunities to whisper lies to us when we are most vulnerable, especially when we are young and wounded. He speaks lies like, "No one will love you after all that you've done…after all that's been done to you." In these wounded places, the lies feel so true they are believed. They find a firm grasp in our minds and are reinforced as we agree with their echoes over the years.

Deeply ingrained lies were at the root of all my negative thoughts and self-contempt. These feelings and beliefs were not from God, and they were destructive. The lies had echoed in my life ever since the period of sexual abuse, but they burrowed further and further into my heart during the years of my eating disorder. While these insidious whispers were just lies, they became my truth because I believed them. However, the Truth comes from what God says about us, "whether or not we want to believe it or 'feel' it to be true."[7]

One lie was so deeply rooted in my heart over the years that it actually became a part of my identity. It began to emerge as I listened to "The Four Streams – How Christ Heals Our Hearts" by John Eldredge.[8] He talked about how the Holy Spirit, as our Counselor, takes the Truth from our heads (an intellectual level) to our innermost beings, our hearts.

Finally, in an encounter with Jesus, the dark lie that was so deeply ingrained in my heart was exposed to the Light (Jesus), allowing me to see it for what it really was. This lie had hindered me from fully, deeply receiving Jesus' love on a heart level. It had affected my ability to believe and receive David's love as well.

This next vision, "The Lie," took me back to an earlier time in my life. I was 15, emotionally at the lowest point in my life, and extremely vulnerable to the Enemy's lies. This encounter became a turning point in the process of my inner healing.

The Lie

Where are we going today?
I wondered
The imagery began
There was more snow
To shovel
Out of my heart

- As I shoveled
A path for Jesus
The scene changed
To my parents' hallway
Going back towards the bedrooms

- Dreading this memory
Knowing it would come
Fear seeping in

- Late at night
A man broke into our house
Face covered and knife in hand
Looking for me
Startled that one of my
Older sisters was there too

- "Fight or flight"
Was NOT my response

- FROZEN

- Silently screaming
Paralyzed with fear
Unable to fight or scream
Like my older sister

- Feeling completely helpless
As he violated us
A stranger who knew my name
The whole experience
So shameful
So degrading

- Out of desperation
I prayed my first prayer
To Jesus
My sister's God

- Begging Him
Not to let this evil man
Rape or kill her
Offering myself in her place

- Years later
Finding out
She had been praying too

- Suddenly
He stopped and left!
There was no reason for him to stop…
He had done so much already
Why stop now?

- Leaving me STUNNED

- My prayer was answered so clearly
Knowing that had to be
God responding
A God I'd never known

- That was the moment
Jesus entered the memory
And swept us away to
"The Journey" path

- Setting me down
I reverted to focusing inward
Dwelling on the negative of my life
Diving was stolen
By severe knee pain
The one thing
I felt created to do
Taken away

- My innocence taken
At nine years old

- Now more shame
Piled on top
Adding to the weight
I was already carrying

- Nothing sacred left
Self-respect
Dignity
Gone

- Numb and apathetic
Depressed
Feeling as though after everything
That had happened in my past
Nothing done to me
Mattered anymore

–We shifted into the heart room
I went into a very dark part
　Of my heart
And pulled out the box
But this time
　　The box was solid black

–Opening the box
　I gave it to Jesus
Who was there with me

–It was completely empty…
Black on the inside too
　Reflecting my heart
　　My life
　My perspective

–The light inside me had gone out
　　Feeling no passion
　　　No purpose in life

–My workout was over
The imagery stopped

　–Stuck

–Having taken on
My 15-year-old mindset
　In my present life

–No desire to seek Jesus
　Or workout

–Two weeks dragged on…

–Feeling apathetic
　Dead inside
Without passion and purpose
　Without worth

–The second Sunday
After being stuck for two weeks
Our Pastor said something unusual
　After his sermon
　"There is someone here
Feeling intense shame"

–My heart pounding…

–"I want you to know
Jesus is not finished with you yet!
　Take His hand again…
There is so much more
He wants to do with you
　On this journey
　　Don't give up"

–His words cut to my heart
As though Jesus said them Himself

–A flame had been relit
　In my heart

–I knew I must
　Press in
And seek Him again…

–That afternoon
　As I began to workout
The imagery picked up
　Right where it left off
After the rescue from the break-in
　Back on "The Journey" path
　　Still feeling apathetic

–Thinking…
*It doesn't matter
What has been done to me
Thinking of the shameful things
　Weighing me down*

–"It does matter!"
　Jesus said

–Then He gave me eyes to see
　My own daughter
　　As though
She had been sexually abused

–My heart shattered…
And in that moment
　I understood
　　It DID matter!

–That day
　I saw a glimpse
Of the Father's heart for ME

"Please take this lie out of my heart!"

Rebecca D. Knight
2009

The Lie — continued

–The scene changed back
To being with Jesus after the break-in

  –Holding my face in His hands
 "I made you
  You are my child…
    I love you!"

 –I replied
"I feel SO UNLOVABLE
I can't even receive Your words"

–I knew He was telling the truth
He did love me…
But in my heart "The Lie"
  Of being unlovable
Was relentless

–"Please take this lie out of my heart!"
  Renouncing it
"Move the truth
  Of Your love
From my head
  Deep into my heart"

–I was unprepared for what came next

  –He reached into my heart
And ripped out the lie

–It was like this root had become
  So entangled around my heart
It had become so much a part of me
  It tore at my heart…heart rending
As it was ripped out

 –The burning pain so real
Searing inside my chest

–Collapsing to my hands and knees
  The intense burning persisted
Then it diminished
   Like smoldering coals
      Until finally subsiding

 –Something magnificent
 Had just taken place
   God moving
 Deep in my heart

  –Rooting out
An invasive, poisonous lie
  Of the enemy

 –Cleansing
Reviving
  Transforming

–No longer numb inside
  Finally, I could FEEL

"*But now, thus says the* LORD, *He who created you, O Jacob, He who formed you, O Israel: 'Fear not, for I have redeemed you; I have called you by name, you are Mine. When you pass through the waters, I will be with you; and through the rivers, they shall not overwhelm you; when you walk through fire you shall not be burned, and the flame shall not consume you. For I am the* LORD, *your God, the Holy One of Israel, your Savior…. Because you are precious in my eyes, and honored, and I love you'*"
(Isaiah 43:1-4 ESV).

"*For you created my inmost being; you knit me together in my mother's womb. I praise you because I am fearfully and wonderfully made; your works are wonderful, I know that full well*"
(Psalm 139:13-14).

"*There is no fear in love, but perfect love casts out fear*"
(I John 4:18 ESV).

CHAPTER NINE

Holy Shower

"Cleanse me with hyssop, and I will be clean; wash me, and I will be whiter than snow"
(Psalm 51:7).

Personal Thoughts

"The Lie" encounter took three weeks to go through because I became absolutely stuck in the middle of it. I reverted to my fifteen-year-old mindset during this time...this was an awful place to get stuck! Perhaps this is why the Lord left this particular memory for last. I was totally unmotivated, numb, and withdrawn as I lost sight of my purpose. All of my passion dissolved into apathy. I had to ask the counselor, "Why am I doing all of this?" I couldn't remember. I stopped getting on the treadmill to seek Jesus. In fact, I stopped exercising altogether.

After I explained to the counselor what had happened during the break-in, he asked me a question. Although I could hear him speaking, I had no idea what he was saying. For some strange reason, I couldn't process his words. I remember that he said I was "dissociating." This had happened to a lesser degree a couple of times before in his office, where my mind had become foggy and it was terribly hard to concentrate and stay engaged in the conversation. But this time was more dramatic. I had no idea what his words meant, and I felt like my mind was in "la-la land," drifting up above me in a strange, surreal dream. I wondered if I was totally "losing it."

At the conclusion of each appointment, David and I would go to lunch and process what the counselor had said. David would carefully explain the counselor's words while I was more coherent and able to take in what had happened. The counselor assured me that it was not unusual for cases like mine to experience this disconnected fogginess.

Looking back, it makes sense to me that "The Lie" of being unlovable had to be completely renounced and removed before I could receive what the Lord had in store for me next. Thankfully, He spoke very clearly through my pastor and cut straight into my heart, relighting the fire within me to seek Him again.

The next vision changed everything. It allowed me to truly feel God's love and to receive it deeply in my heart, instead of just knowing it in my head.

"I felt shame washing away."

Holy Shower

The imagery began
  Climbing UP
The mountainous journey path
  Jesus leading the way

 – The scene changed
I found myself in a
  Holy Shower
Raining from Heaven

 – Darkness surrounded me
  Except
Beautiful white sparkling water
  Like snow shining in the sun
Reflecting light
  Raining down from Heaven
    On my hands
      Warm and inviting
SO BEAUTIFUL
Drawing me more deeply in

 – I felt SHAME
  Washing away…

 – This Holy Shower was
  Radically different
Than the long showers I used to take
  Trying to feel clean
    But never could

 – This beautiful water
Was washing me
  INSIDE
Deep down inside

– Only Jesus' blood can do this!

 – I felt …
  Pure
    Clean
      Beautiful
For the first time in my life
  Being naked and unashamed

 – Looking deeper into the water
  I saw Jesus
  Dying on the cross
    His eyes filled with love
  Looking at me

 – I was the JOY
Set before Him
  As He endured the cross!

– Incomprehensible
  – WHY?

 – Suffering
  Such agony
For sinful people
    For ME?

 – His glory displayed
  Such love
Such grace!

 – I had NEVER
Felt like this
  Before

"I will sprinkle clean water on you, and you will be clean; I will cleanse you from all your impurities and from all your idols" (Ezekiel 36:25).

"Therefore, since we are surrounded by such a great cloud of witnesses, let us throw off everything that hinders and the sin that so easily entangles. And let us run with perseverance the race marked out for us, fixing our eyes on Jesus, the pioneer and perfecter of faith. For the joy set before Him He endured the cross, scorning its shame, and sat down at the right hand of the throne of God. Consider Him who endured such opposition from sinners, so that you will not grow weary and lose heart" (Hebrews 12:1-3).

CHAPTER TEN

My Beloved

"You have stolen My heart, My sister, My Bride; you have stolen My heart with one glance of your eyes, with one jewel of your necklace"
(Song of Songs 4:9).

Personal Thoughts

The "Holy Shower" was so beautiful. It left me with a resounding sense of joy for a couple of days. In the waters of grace, I tangibly felt my shame and the filth of my past wash away—both the sins done to me, as well as my sinful responses. For the first time in my life, I felt pure, clean and beautiful both inside and out—fresh and innocent in the sight of God. I no longer had anything to hide. The experience was indescribable. Instead of believing in Jesus just intellectually, I encountered His love and grace on a deep heart level, leaving me in absolute awe.

As I journaled about the "Holy Shower," I gazed out at the Michigan winter snow. The sun appeared from behind the dreary grayness and sparkled across the shimmering snow as it fell from the sky. Tears flowed as I was struck by the beautiful memory of the "Holy Shower." Gratefulness flooded my heart. In only an hour, so much had changed. I'd gone from being stuck in the darkest pit of my life to experiencing an unexpected, eminent joy from the "Holy Shower."

The next vision replayed the "Holy Shower" and then moved on to something breathtaking and new. I could no longer see Jesus dying on the cross, although the "Holy Shower" continued to rain down on me from Heaven. Through the shower, I could now see the resurrected Lord reaching His hand out for me, beckoning me towards Him.

"Never have I felt love like this."

My Beloved

The risen Jesus
Held out His hand
For me

- Taking His hand
He slowly
Pulled me out of the Holy Shower

- The sparkling water
Clung to my body
Clothing me in a
Shimmering white wedding dress

- As the veil
Covered my head
I knew it was His righteousness

- Becoming
The Bride of Christ
His Beloved!

- Kneeling before Him
Heart in my hands
I felt compelled
To give it to Him
To present all of me
To Him
Once again

- He pulled me up
Drawing me
Close to Him

- We walked together
Hand in hand
To the top of His mountain
Overlooking His glorious creation
A breathtaking site of beauty

- But what He delighted in
Most of all
Out of ALL His creation
Was ME
His Bride!

- He couldn't take His eyes off me!
They sparkled
My heart melted

- NEVER
Had I felt love like this
In my innermost being
Deep in my heart

*"Let the King be enthralled
by your beauty; honor Him,
for He is your Lord"*
(Psalm 45:11).

CHAPTER ELEVEN

Wholehearted

"To Him who is able to keep you from stumbling and to present you before His glorious presence without fault and with great joy"
(Jude 1:24).

Personal Thoughts

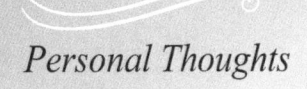

After experiencing "My Beloved," my rapturous, unbridled joy lasted even longer than the soothing bliss following the "Holy Shower." I thought of Moses coming down off Mount Sinai after meeting with God "…with his face shining" (Exodus 34:29 ESV). I don't know if my face was shining, but I felt the radiance of God flowing out of me as I described this encounter to David.

During my journal time, I reflected on all that had happened – the loving way Jesus entered into the four darkest memories of my life and rescued me. He transformed those memories forever, making them beautiful, giving me beauty for ashes. He showed me that His deep love had always been available, but now I was able to receive it. Although these visions flashed across my mind frequently, I continued to re-read my journal, desperate not to forget any detail.

I read the Psalms frequently during this three-month period of inner healing. Some of the verses jumped out at me because I felt like I had just personally experienced what was written there. Verses I knew from other parts of the Bible came to mind as well, and as I wrote these in my journal, they became a part of my story too.

I couldn't imagine any more visions coming after I had experienced "My Beloved," but I continued to seek Jesus, praising Him for all He had done in my heart. Yet there was more – there is always more with Him!

The next vision was like a wonderful review of all four rescues as He entered into each dark memory, gathering up the pieces of my broken heart and putting me back together. This new encounter left me with a deep feeling of wholeness.

"He heals the brokenhearted and binds up their wounds" (Psalm 147:3).

"I felt so loved…so complete."

Wholehearted

The rescue imagery
Precious to me
Each traumatic memory
Now a rescue
Where Jesus came
Sweeping me away
Changing the memory
FOREVER

– The imagery began
Recalling
Each of the four rescues
The Sexual Abuse
The Break-In
The Eating Disorder
The Accident

– He was gathering up
All the wounded parts of me
Putting me back together
In His arms

– Instead of watching
From behind
I suddenly became the woman
In His arms

– Then He breathed into me
His breath of life

– Being carried in His arms
No longer felt
Like a place of rescue

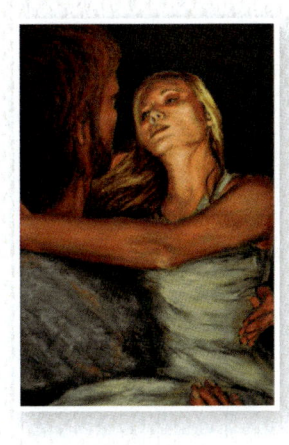

– But one of a bride
Being held by her groom
Very intimate

– He twirled me around
A couple of times
In JOY!

– Finally
He lifted me up
Presenting me holy and blameless
To the Father

– It was finished

– I felt so loved
So complete
Overflowing with JOY and PEACE
Having experienced
His GRACE and GLORY

"*For the L*ORD *will take delight in you.... As a bridegroom rejoices over his bride, so will your God rejoice over you*" (Isaiah 62:4b-5).

"*Husbands, love your wives, just as Christ loved the church and gave Himself up for her to make her holy, cleansing her by the washing with water through the Word, and to present her to Himself as a radiant church, without stain or wrinkle or any other blemish, but holy and blameless*" (Ephesians 5:25-27).

CHAPTER TWELVE

A Transformed Heart

*"Whoever believes in Me,
as Scripture has said, rivers of living water
will flow from within them"*
(John 7:38).

Personal Thoughts

After Jesus gathered the pieces of my broken past and put me back together, fully binding up my broken heart, I felt completely healed. I felt whole. After my healing, I had an extreme desire to paint these visions all over my walls so I could remember them in perfect clarity. Sadly, I had never had even one art class to teach me how to paint and felt completely unqualified to attempt such an undertaking.

I wondered if others needed to know that Jesus could transform and heal dark memories of past wounds. In nearly 30 years of Bible study and going to church, I had never heard of anything like this before. I desired to pass on what I had received to other wounded hearts, so I rewrote my journal entries into a book. My words felt so incomplete without pictures of the visions that in discouragement, I put the book on a shelf. It occurred to me that maybe I could find an artist to paint a few of the visions for me.

Part way through my journey, a vision in my heart room began to appear intermittently and gradually evolved over the course of the rescues. This vision came to me between rescues and almost seemed like a period of rest – a time of just being in the Lord's presence in my heart. The visual beauty of the transformation of my heart room inspired me. This room was a place where I wanted to spend time with Jesus.

"Jesus is so pleased with you."

A Transformed Heart

Snow has disappeared
From my heart

- Part way through
My journey
A change began to take place

- At times
I found myself in
My heart room
Without snow

- Sitting by a campfire
With Jesus
Leaning into
His shoulder and chest
Just being together
Peaceful
So Peaceful…

- A period of relief
Of rest
Between rescues

- When snow appeared
It was time to press on
With the journey
More healing was needed

- Later
A beautiful fountain
Sprang up
Deeper in my heart
Forming a river
That ran behind us

- Having seen this fountain
years before
In my mind
During a prayer
It came with special meaning

- Amy's pastor
Praying for me,
A discouraged mom
With preschool children
He said, "Jesus is
So pleased with you.
He knows the intentions
Of your heart."

- I remember crying
Feeling so inadequate
To train my daughters

- This beautiful fountain
And those words
Touched me deeply that day

A Transformed Heart – continued

- When the fountain
Appeared in my heart again
It came with the memory
Of those sweet words
"Jesus is so pleased with you"
Bringing a smile
To my face

- A garden
Began to form
And grow around us

- My heart was coming alive
No longer a cold, barren cave
With only snow

- Beautiful
Peaceful
Warm and cozy
By the fire with Him

- A fleeting image
Sitting on His lap
On the throne

- Remembering
Multicolored light radiating
From "The Box"
At His feet

- He was transforming
My shattered, broken heart
Of stone
Into treasure

- What is this
Colorful treasure
Streaming from "The Box?"

- Suddenly, He threw
The contents of "The Box"
Into the campfire
In my heart room

- They now appeared as
Sparkling gems
Giving the fire
Radiant colors
At the base

- Extraordinary beauty

- Once gray and lifeless
Cold and hard
Broken rocks

- Now gems
ALIVE
Reflecting glorious colors
In the fire
Of my heart

- My treasure
A transformed heart
Fully alive to Jesus

- Reflecting
His extraordinary beauty
Displaying His splendor

- Desire stirs
The time is right
To go down the mountain
And encourage others
To seek the Good Shepherd
On their own journey
To the High Places

- There is more He wants to do
SO MUCH MORE
Than I ever dreamed possible!

- Dear reader
Do not be afraid
Take hold of
His hand…
There's more for you too!

"*Y*ou are a garden locked up, My sister, My bride; you are a spring enclosed, a sealed fountain" (Song of Songs 4:12).

"*Y*ou will be like a well-watered garden, like a spring whose waters never fail" (Isaiah 58:11b).

"*B*ut we have this treasure in jars of clay to show that this all-surpassing power is from God and not from us" (2 Corinthians 4:7).

CHAPTER THIRTEEN

Leaning In

"Who is this coming up from the wilderness leaning on her Beloved?"
(Song of Songs 8:5).

Personal Thoughts

After a few months of searching for a painter, my pursuit seemed futile, and my book remained on the shelf. Moving on with my life, I joined a prayer training class at my church in hopes of becoming a part of the prayer team. A woman walked in and began to talk. "I have this picture in my mind of God, and He is sitting in front of a large white canvas. It's completely blank, but it's like He wants to paint something." My heart began to pound. "Does this mean anything to any of you?" she continued.

Emotion welled up, and I immediately began to share a bit of my story: I told of my deep desire to paint the visions the Lord had given me but acknowledged my lack of training and skill. In fact, I had never taken an art class. The group spontaneously circled around me and began to pray, essentially anointing me as a painter. I felt a mild burning in my chest during the prayer time, and one woman in the group said she felt like her hands were on fire. After class, another woman came up to me and said that she kept seeing the word *chalk* in her mind during the prayer time (which sounded a bit crazy to me) and that she felt like she was supposed to tell me.

Not knowing where to begin, I signed up for a painting class that worked on independent projects. I explained to the instructor what type of images I wanted to learn to paint. He suggested I start with pastels, which he further explained were made of soft chalk. A wave of excitement swept over me. I knew God was at work! This was the beginning of an eight-year process, the results of which you now hold in your hands.

None of the paintings reveal the exact vision that the Lord showed me; however, each one in succession represents the vision more clearly. For example, the painting of Jesus on the throne with the little girl on His lap looks very different from the vision I received in my mind. However, I was able to capture a certain degree of His tenderness, so it seemed important to include. Perhaps someday a revision will come.

After the inner healing was complete, a special vision began to appear repeatedly in my mind. It often returns during difficult circumstances or trials – the storms in my life. This new vision of "Leaning In" came to me for the first time when I wasn't even working out, which was unusual but encouraging because I couldn't exercise at the time due to joint pain. I have learned over time that "Leaning In" is a place I can go to in my mind at any time. This painting represents my special place with Jesus and takes me to the eye of the storm, close to Jesus' heart, leaning in to Him. His peace washes over me and calms my heart with the knowledge that He is in control of everything and He is good. Even when I don't understand His ways, I can still trust in Him.

The most memorable trial during this time came when I was diagnosed with lupus toward the end of my painting years. I found myself leaning in to Him often. At the beginning of my journey, I felt like the bleeding woman in the Bible who reached out to touch Jesus' garment for healing, but I could never quite grab hold. By the end of the journey, I felt that I could finally reach the hem of His garment to receive His healing touch. When I was diagnosed, I was in the middle of painting "Healed," a depiction of myself as the bleeding woman who was finally taking hold of Jesus' precious garment. Leaning in to Him became a comfort and encouragement to me as I painted with my aching body.

"His peace pouring into my heart."

Leaning In

Storms
Of tribulation
   Swirl wildly
About me

- Suddenly
    I'm leaning in to Jesus
Close to His heart
   Almost hearing
His heartbeat

- Feeling safe in His arms
Like the little girl
   In His lap on the throne
     He is tender with me

- His peace
Pouring into my heart
Standing close to
   My Beloved
Knowing He is in control
   Of everything
He is the eye of the storm

- He can be trusted
His good
Will be evident
   In the end

- Purpose in trials
Deep
Spiritual purpose

- My old self
The bleeding woman
   Healed at last

- Not only touching
Jesus' garment
But now being held
   In His arms
    As His Beloved

- What began
With Amy's Hug
Finished
   With His embrace!

- Everything in my past
   Was worth experiencing
For deep intimacy
   With Jesus

- My Savior
My Lord
My Beloved!

- The image changes
   Now David's arms
Embrace me
My loving husband

- He sways me
Back and forth
   A slow dance begins

- Selflessly holding me
   All these years
Through the emotional trials
   Of my life

- Standing by me
Every step of the way

- Faithful and true...
   So many years
Loving me
   A challenge
He was designed for

- Long ago
   David was given
A glimpse
   Of my "glory self"
    Who God created me to be

- He has loved me
   With grace and patience
Cords of kindness
Ties of love
Perseverance

- Loving me
   Into that person

- Although transformation
Comes from the Lord...
   I realize
God has loved me
   Through David

- Gratefulness and love
   For my husband
    Well up
Overflowing

Leaning In — *continued*

–The love of my life
   Here on earth
My husband
   My intimate friend

–More than
   I could hope for
     A gift
From above

–Now that I'm
   wholehearted
Our marriage has a chance
   To be all God intended

–A memory of our wedding
Flashes across my mind

–A sacred union
Ordained by God

–As we kneel before Jesus
Light of the world
   He gives us His light

–Shining brightly now
   His Holy Spirit
In our hearts

–Awareness heightened
   We are in a battle
Our marriage – a target
   A threat to the enemy
Who desires to
   Steal, kill and destroy

–Sensing Jesus' arms
Now seeing His full armor
   Around both of us
   His warrior
     And warrior bride

–He is our refuge
Our strong tower
   Where we must run
When attacked
Under the shelter
   Of His wings

–He is the eye of the storm

"Everything in heaven and earth is Yours. Yours, LORD, is the kingdom; You are exalted as head over all" (1 Chronicles 29:11b).

"But the LORD's unfailing love surrounds the one who trusts in Him" (Psalm 32:10b).

"You will keep in perfect peace those whose minds are steadfast, because they trust in You" (Isaiah 26:3).

"I led them with cords of human kindness, with ties of love" (Hosea 11:4).

"A large crowd followed and pressed around Him. And a woman was there who had been subject to bleeding for twelve years. She had suffered a great deal under the care of many doctors and had spent all she had, yet instead of getting better she grew worse. When she heard about Jesus, she came up behind Him in the crowd and touched His cloak, because she thought, 'If I just touch His clothes, I will be healed.' Immediately her bleeding stopped and she felt in her body that she was freed from her suffering.

At once Jesus realized that power had gone out from Him. He turned around in the crowd and asked, 'Who touched My clothes?'

'You see the people crowding against You,' His disciples answered, 'and yet You can ask, ' "Who touched Me?" '

But Jesus kept looking around to see who had done it. Then the woman, knowing what had happened to her, came and fell at His feet and, trembling with fear, told Him the whole truth. He said to her, 'Daughter, your faith has healed you. Go in peace and be freed from your suffering' " (Mark 5:24-34).

Healed

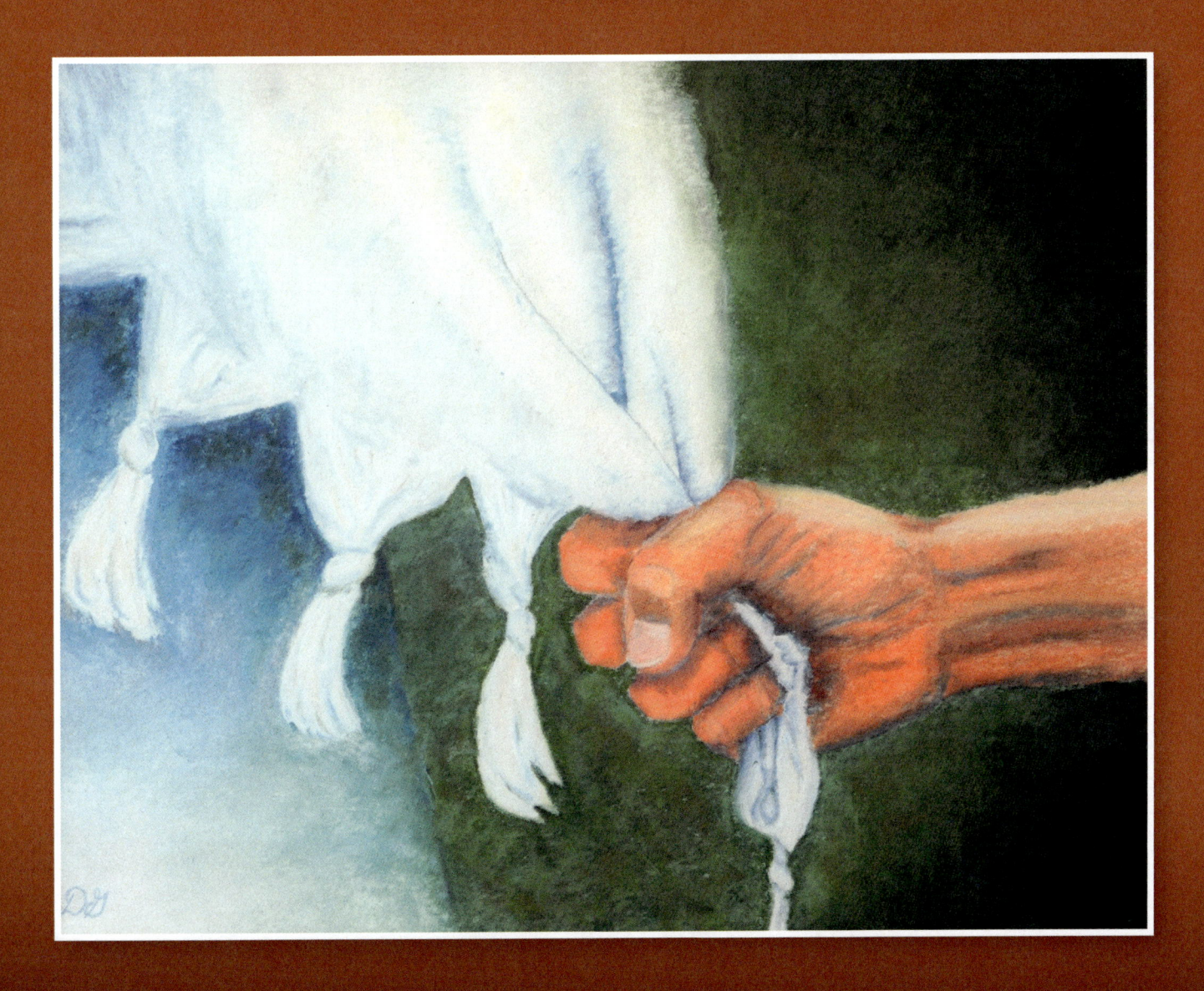

CHAPTER FOURTEEN

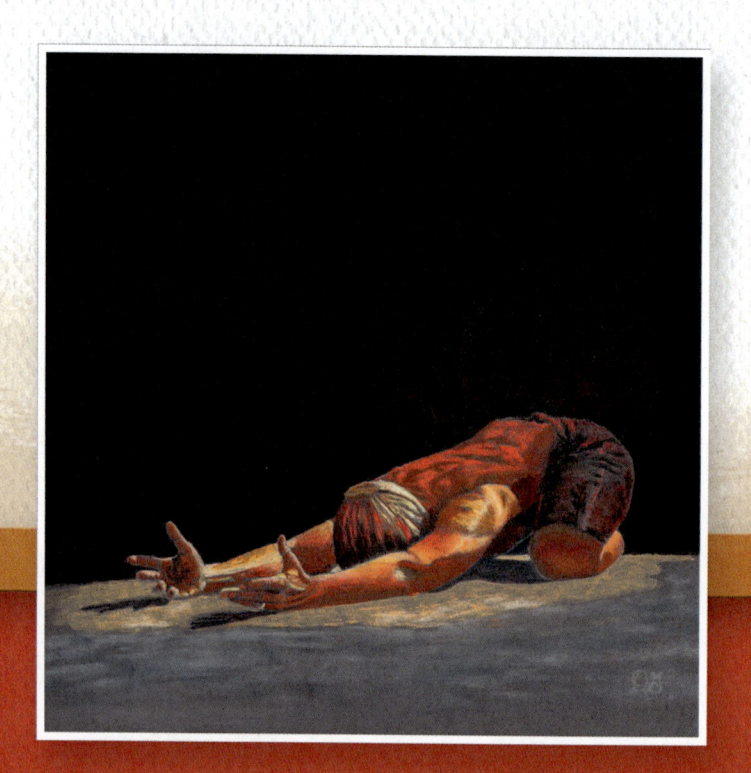

His Golden Girl

*"But He knows the way that I take;
when He has tested me, I will come forth as gold"*
(Job 23:10).

Personal Thoughts

After five years of basking in my inner healing and letting it seep deeply into my heart through painting, the trial of lupus entered my life. This trial directly touched several vulnerable areas all at once, reviving deep struggles of the past I thought I had overcome. The effects of the lupus began to reveal things in my heart that disturbed me greatly. I found myself back in a fiery trial that was agonizingly difficult and increasingly intense. It became clear that I had to surrender daily and die to self even more than I had in the past.

Although the race marked out for each of us is different and the trials will vary from person to person, I'm beginning to think the process we must all go through is similar if we want to truly be a disciple of Jesus and follow Him. I described my struggle to Amy, feeling as though I were in the Refiner's fire. She had an immediate response. She remembered when our local newspaper had called me the "Golden Girl" after I had won the Pan American Games in diving many years before. She said, "God is bringing what happened in the physical to pass now in the spiritual realm." He was making me His Golden Girl! It was a beautiful thought, which touched and encouraged me deeply.

After Amy's words, I immediately recalled a song by Misty Edwards called "Fling Wide."[9] I remembered praying that song with all my heart after the Lord completed my inner healing. I wanted the Lord to have His way with me, whatever that looked like. My diagnosis of lupus had come on the heels of that prayer.

In the midst of that fire, I sensed the presence of the Holy Spirit and felt a deep resolve within, knowing what I must do. I knew I must fix my eyes and mind on Jesus, cling to Him, trust Him, and fully surrender to Him in the fire. There was no other place to go.

I am still a work in process. Aren't we all? I still have a tendency to slip back into this struggle on occasion, but my times of weakness are less frequent with each passing day. I want to be His Golden Girl and to have Him say to me when I reach Heaven, "Well done, good and faithful servant" (Matthew 25:21). Don't you?

"Full surrender...dying to self."

His Golden Girl

Fling Wide, *by Misty Edwards*

Awake, Awake O North Wind
Awake, Awake O South Wind
Blow over me
Come O winds of testing
Come winds of refreshing
Blow over me
Let the winds blow
Let the winds blow
Fling wide
The door into my soul
Open up the door into my heart
Have Your way
I won't be afraid
I will face the wind
I won't be afraid
I'll embrace the flame
Let the winds blow
Let the winds blow
Take me through the fire
Take me through the rain,
Take me through the testing
I'll do anything
Test me, try me, prove me, refine me
Like the gold, like the gold

The Refiner's Fire
  Miserable
    Humbling
Unrelenting
Sorrow and suffering

  – Painfully submitting
    Seeking Him
In the fire
  Not seeing or sensing
    His presence
      At first

– Under the pressure
  Of His heavy hand
The fiery furnace
  Cranks hotter

  – A consuming fire
Unbearable

– Enduring the fire admirably
  Impossible
  Without Him

  – The Refiner
Brings up
  Dross
To skim off
  My heart

– Seeking Him again
  Deeper in the fire
More desperate to find Him

– Quietly discovering
  He is near
Walking through the fire
  With me

– Giving courage
Power to face
  The ugliness of self
Rising to the surface

  – Sin
Hidden idols
  Strongholds
Ugliness revealed
  Overwhelming

– Oblivious
That it was there
  Until now
Clearly seen

– Broken
  At the end of
    Self

– Deeper surrender
Humiliated by my cycle of failure
  Falling in a heap
    Of serious repentance
At the foot
  Of the cross

  – The only place
    Of hope

His Golden Girl – continued

– Taking greater notice
   Of Jesus
     God of the universe
       Innocent…without sin
Suffering my punishment
   Dying
   For me!

– My trial in this fire
Pales in comparison
   To what He endured
   Leading up to
     And on
     The cross

– He even prayed for mercy
   For those
     Killing Him?

– Unimaginable
His love and forgiveness
   Beyond understanding

– Although undeserving
His grace washes over me
   His blood
Poured out on the cross
   Cleanses the filth
   Shame
    Sin
From the inside out

– Covering me with
   His purity
   His Holiness

His Righteousness
   Creating in me
   A clean heart

– Forgiveness granted
   His Love and mercy
   Displayed
     In all His glory

– I reach out
Embracing Him
   On a deeper
     Heart level

– Gratefulness overwhelming
   Tears flow
     Unhindered

– Jesus' mysterious work
   Purifying
   Purposeful
Revealing deeper insight
   Into His heart
And my wretchedness
   Weaknesses
   Vulnerability
     To go astray

– Realizing even more
My great need
   Of Him
   Moment by moment

– The Holy Spirit
Rises up
   In power

In that place
   Of full surrender
     Dying to self

– In the midst of the storm
   Jesus says
   "Take courage! It is I
   Don't be afraid"

– Courage is needed
To step out of the boat
   Out of my
   Comfort zone

– "Come," He beckons
   As I step out of the boat
He enables me
   To walk slowly
Laboriously
Through the storm
   On holy ground

– Eyes fixed on Him
And Him alone
   Following
   Clinging

– More desperately dependent
   More fully obedient
Or I would sink
   Like Peter on the water

– The storm
Turns back to the Refiner's fire
   Noticing now
   The fire burned up
   Ropes of bondage

    Releasing me
From captivity
    Freedom

– His "good"
Conforming me
    Closer to the image
      Of Jesus

– When the Refiner
Finally sees His reflection
    In the liquid metal
      Of my heart
The process is complete
For now
    With this trial

– The likeness
Of Jesus Himself
    More clearly evident
In my heart
    Displaying
Fruit of the Spirit
    In greater measure

– There was a time
When the local newspaper
    Called me
      "Golden Girl"
For diving

– But now
The Lord is molding me closer
    Into what He truly
Created me to be

    His Golden Girl
Reflecting His image
    His character

– Peace surpassing understanding
    Fullness of joy
    In His presence
Gratefulness overflowing
    Intimacy
With my Lord and Savior
    My Beloved
Jesus

– The refining process in the crucible
    Never fully complete
Until Heaven
    Knowing more will come
      Down the road

– Yet…Never the same
After the current fiery process
    is complete
Giving trials and suffering
Deeper spiritual purpose
    Greater understanding
      Realizing
    We need trials

– To become
More like Jesus
    Pure gold

– To know Him
More intimately
    His heart of love
For us

"But the fruit of the Spirit is love, joy, peace, patience, kindness, goodness, faithfulness, gentleness, self-control; against such things there is no law" (Galatians 5:22-23 ESV).

"Take away the dross from the silver, and the smith has material for a vessel" (Proverbs 25:4 ESV).

CHAPTER FIFTEEN

My Greatest Rescue

"He generously poured out the Spirit upon us through Jesus Christ our Savior"
(Titus 3:6 NLT).

Personal Thoughts

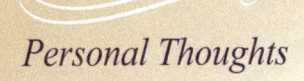

The realization of my greatest rescue became evident when talking with a close friend after she read my rough draft. I had not included this chapter in the book. However, it became clear as we talked that it was an essential turning point of my life and part of the story. If this rescue had never taken place, none of the others would have either, and I'm not sure I'd be alive today. I certainly would not be living the abundant life I am now. Looking back, I now see what a pivotal and critical rescue this was.

As a disinterested teenager, I did not recognize God's intervention in my life at first. He delivered me from my sexual abuser, my coach, by allowing a painful, incurable condition in my knees when I was fifteen. I was forced to quit diving. Mixed emotions filled my heart. I was extremely relieved to be free from my abuser, but diving meant everything to me. I was devastated. My life's dream—to go away to college on a diving scholarship and someday make the Olympic Team—had been stolen from me. I didn't believe in God at all during this time of my life. The following verse describes me in that place:

"They are darkened in their understanding, alienated from the life of God because of the ignorance that is in them, due to their hardness of heart" (Ephesians 4:18 ESV).

God got my attention by answering my first prayer during the break-in when an intruder was about to rape my sister. Even though I felt like my sister's God had answered my prayer by causing the man to suddenly stop and leave the house, I still hit rock bottom afterward. It felt like more shame was piled on top of the load I was already carrying. Although I couldn't deny that there might be a God, I had the perspective that IF there was a God, He certainly didn't love me. Maybe He loved my sister, but not me. Why would He let all of the sexual abuse happen if He loved me? Nevertheless, I started going to a Young Life (YL) Club because I enjoyed playing ping pong with one of the leaders. My coach hated God, and going to Club also gave me a weird satisfaction by making

"Something took ahold of me, and I really listened."

— Denise Yater

him angry. He couldn't control me anymore, and that felt good. Then something happened that absolutely shocked me. My atheistic dad not only suggested I go to YL Camp that summer, but he actually paid my way. We had hosted a YL Club in our house on occasion because of one of my older sisters. Because my dad was impressed with the YL leaders and what good role models they were, he probably thought it would be good for me to go to camp.

Even though I wasn't interested in God, I had to admit, YL Camp was amazing. I was able to participate in everything (except the hike) despite my knees. They had awesome activities like tubing down an extremely cold river, horseback riding, enjoying the top of a mountain on a wild jeep ride, playing ping pong, and looking at more stars than I'd ever seen in my life. The energy level at YL Club each night during camp was off the chart, and the speaker was very thought-provoking. His dad unexpectedly passed away early in the week, which profoundly affected the entire camp. Something took ahold of me, and I really listened.

After hearing the story of Jesus for the first time, it seemed too good to be true. IF the story was true, I definitely wanted to know Him! He was a lot different than how I pictured God. For the second time in my life, I clearly remember praying. I prayed with all my heart under the magnificent Colorado stars during the 20 minutes of time alone they gave us, "Jesus, if you are real, I want to know You. Please show me You are REAL!" As I looked at the stars, it was easy to believe in a Creator. "The heavens declare the glory of God; the skies proclaim the work of His hands" (Psalm 19:1). But after years of abuse and unbelief, I needed something more personal to know that He really cared about ME before I was ready to surrender my life and follow Him.

About two weeks after YL Camp, my knees were completely and miraculously healed. The swelling resolved, and there was no pain at all! The doctor couldn't explain it. During the 18 months I endured swollen knees, a new diving coach had been hired, an Olympic medalist, and a new facility with platforms had been built in town. I went to this new pool and just stood there for a minute, gathering my courage to talk to a coach I had never met before. He walked over, seeming to know who I was, and asked if I wanted to dive. My face lit up and I nodded yes! He was so welcoming! I immediately changed into my suit and joined in the practice. I knew God had restored my knees and put diving back into my life, resurrecting my passion and life dream.

After I heard about Jesus at YL Camp and personally experienced His power of physical healing in my knees, I knew He was real. More than that, He seemed to care about me. With a sweet nudge from a friend on my high school's gymnastics team, I began to follow Jesus.

Why Jesus entered my life at all is a mystery to me, but looking back, it was also my **greatest rescue**. "For He has rescued us [me] from the dominion of darkness and brought us [me] into the kingdom of the Son He loves..." (Colossians 1:13). At the time, I didn't understand the meaning of the physical pain that had forced me to quit diving, but the Lord used this season off to bring about deep spiritual change. When my knees prevented me from diving, He used a high school YL Camp to open my eyes to Him.

Years later, when I was unable to dive due to the back injury in college caused by my motorcycle accident, the Lord gave me an opportunity to be a part of His rescue of another lost and hurting teenager at another YL Camp. "We love because He first loved us." (1 John 4:19). The experience was surreal. I got to pass on to her the things I had learned and received from my own times of trial, and it gave me an excitement that I had never felt before. Sharing my story with this suicidal teenager and watching the Lord change her life through it gave me a deeper meaning

My Greatest Rescue – continued

and purpose in life, far beyond diving. YL Camp had such an impact on me that I introduced David to it and we remained involved with it, even years after our own kids had grown up and gone off to college.

I now have a strong stirring in my heart to share with others what the Lord gave to me through this inner healing experience. I knew Jesus had the power of healing, but I never considered that He would heal past wounds and memories, especially when some of them took place before I knew Him. He compelled me to paint, to write out this story, and to pass on what He has done. I have met so many wounded people who need the Lord's healing touch in the deep places of their hearts. Are you one of them? There is SO MUCH MORE He wants to do with you, too!

"Blessed be the God and Father of our Lord Jesus Christ, the Father of mercies and God of all comfort, who comforts us in all our affliction, so that we may be able to comfort those who are in any affliction, with the comfort with which we ourselves are comforted by God. For as we share abundantly in Christ's sufferings, so through Christ we share abundantly in comfort too" (2 Corinthians 1:3-5 ESV).

My deepest desire and prayer is that the Lord will use my paintings, story, and writings to be a catalyst for you as you enter into your own personal journey of healing with the Good Shepherd. Is He reaching His hand out for you? Will you take it? Be courageous – it is SO WORTH IT! "Be strong and courageous Do not be afraid; do not be discouraged, for the LORD your God is with you wherever you go" (Joshua 1:9).

After my greatest rescue, a long process took place before deep inner healing came. Perhaps I needed to mature spiritually enough to understand what His Word was saying to me. My lack of understanding led me to areas that tripped me up for far too long. I had to process and learn many things from Bible studies over the years. Once healing began, it brought many things I had learned in the past to light. Perhaps the Holy Spirit moved truth from my head to my heart, where it had a much deeper impact.

I long to share the insights gained from my healing process with those who have wounded and/or hardened hearts. Another book is in the planning stages to help my readers gain some understanding from my long journey that will shorten their healing process or give insight into the next step if they become stuck. In the meantime, I invite you to listen to my Retreat Talks for a few key "next steps" of application for your own journey (see pg. 100).

I can tell you without a doubt, there is great hope for healing, freedom, and transformation through Jesus if you don't give up. However, you must have ears to really hear the message, an open heart to receive the truth, and perseverance to continue until you fully understand and are willing to submit. Then your heart will be transformed by the power of God in His perfect timing.

Clearly, from reading my story, you know that it wasn't smooth sailing after "My Greatest Rescue." Sometimes it felt like I was hanging onto a thread for dear life, but looking back, I think Jesus held onto me during those times. I dare not think of what would have happened without Him. Deep down, I knew Jesus was the key to everything I desired. He knew me completely, sins and all, but He still wanted me and loved me deeply. He was faithful, trustworthy, and promised to always be with me. He would never leave me. He was what I was missing in life. He was (and is) the ultimate source of the joy, peace, hope, love, and healing that I so desired. He has completely and beautifully transformed me and my heart over years of pursuing Him.

I am overwhelmingly grateful for God's work in my life. I would willingly go through everything in my past again to receive the intimacy I now have with Jesus. He has redeemed all of my past! "He has made everything beautiful in its time" (Ecclesiastes 3:11). There is nothing more important than knowing Him. He is my Savior, my Lord, and my Beloved. He is my Deliverer, my Healer, my Stronghold, my Refuge, my Hope, my Comforter, my Peace, my Joy, and my God—no matter what is going on in the circumstances of life. He was sent to give us all abundant life.

"The thief comes only to steal and kill and destroy. I (Jesus) came that they may have life and have it abundantly"
(John 10:10 ESV).

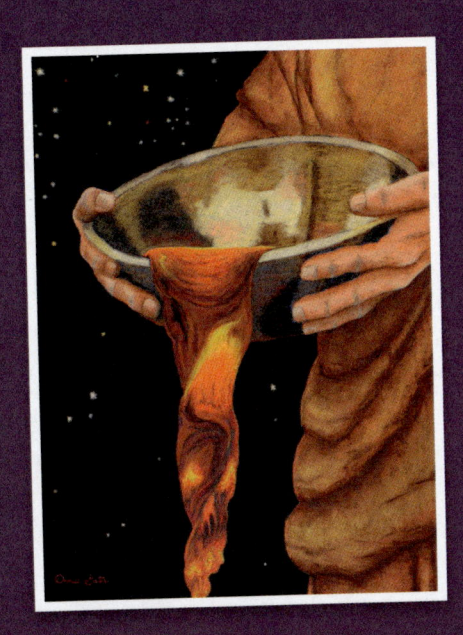

"The Spirit of the Sovereign Lord is on Me, because the Lord has anointed Me to preach good news to the poor. He has sent Me to bind up the brokenhearted, to proclaim freedom for the captives and release from darkness for the prisoners, to proclaim the year of the Lord's favor and the day of vengeance of our God, to comfort all who mourn, and provide for those who grieve in Zion; to bestow on them a crown of beauty instead of ashes, the oil of gladness instead of mourning, and a garment of praise instead of a spirit of despair. They will be called oaks of righteousness, a planting of the Lord for the display of His splendor"
(Isaiah 61:1-3).

"In the last days, God says, I will pour out my Spirit on all people. Your sons and daughters will prophesy, your young men will see visions, your old men will dream dreams. Even on my servants, both men and women, I will pour out my Spirit in those days, and they will prophesy"
(Acts 2:17-18).

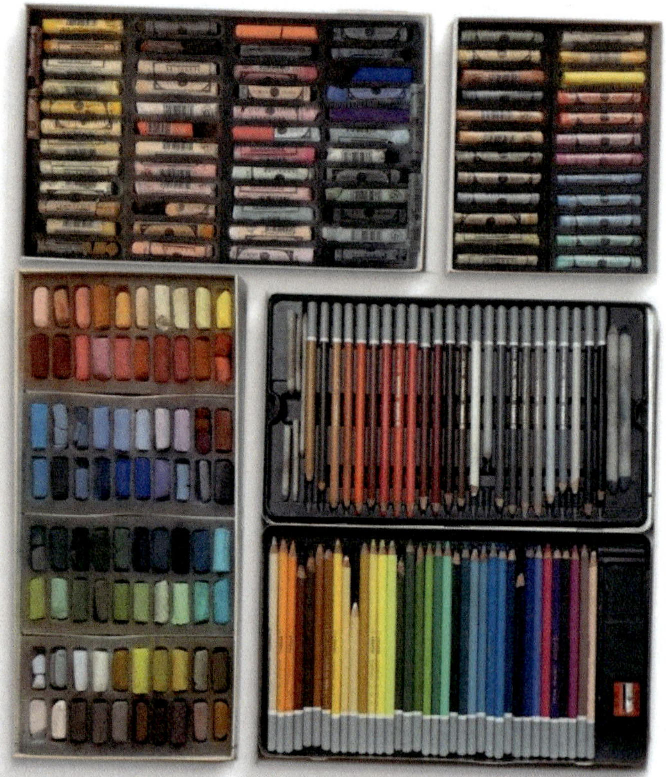

Acknowledgments

An amazing group of people surrounded, encouraged, and prayed for me as this challenging project came to life. It has been a team effort. Each person played a part to enhance the whole. They gave their time and expertise to help others who needed hope and healing in their lives. I am so grateful for each of those who participated with me in their own way.

My Family

I am especially thankful to my own family. My husband David has supported me and walked through life with me for over 30 years as he fought for my heart through bold and loving prayers. Knowing that he was powerless to fix me, he still chose to love me, encourage me, walk alongside me, hold me as I cried, and pray for me through it all. He never gave up on me, even when I was a mess. He remained always positive and uplifting, pointing out lies in my thinking and helping me to replace them with truth. I am so grateful he went with me to all of the counseling sessions and helped me process what happened after each one. I also appreciate his support to go to a Christian counselor our insurance didn't cover. In addition, he encouraged me to pursue painting lessons, buy supplies, frame the paintings, mount large prints of my paintings on Gatorboard to share at retreats, as well as hire a graphic artist and editor to put the finishing touches on this book. Although it has been a costly endeavor, he said, "It's been worth every cent."

My daughter Felicia spent countless hours editing my rough draft and helped bring more clarity to the story. My thoughts have a tendency to jump around, but she was able to gently bring my thoughts together in a more cohesive way so others would be able to follow the story more easily. Like my husband, she has been able to see through the muck and mire and pull out the true meaning of what I have attempted to share. It also took boldness and patience on her part to work with me on such a tender subject. What a gift she has been to me in pulling this story together.

My mother, Dolores, gave me many hugs as I began to share my story. Putting myself in her shoes, I'm sure it was uncomfortable to have made it public. My dad has passed away, although I have no doubt he knows what I am doing and is grateful to Jesus for healing me. As hard as it was to share this book with my mom, I am grateful with how she has responded and embraced me through it. She knows I am compelled to share openly in order to help others who have hidden away the darkness and shame of their own wounds because they don't know what else to do. I believe she has come to accept my story of healing as a gift from the Lord, and I pray He continues to give her His peace. To be very clear, my past sexual abuse was not my parents' fault, and I do not blame them in any way. They didn't know. My biggest regret is that I didn't tell them right away. My coach had tremendous control over me, and honestly, it didn't even occur to me that telling them was an option.

I look up to my sister Amy as a spiritual mentor, even though she is younger than me. She has always been there for me, especially in hard times. I am continually drawn to Jesus more deeply by seeing the intimacy she has with Him. Her prayers have shown me His power, increased my faith immensely, and even taught me to pray more boldly and listen more intently. I have loved all of the music CDs (especially *Passion: Our Love Is Loud*) and sermons she has sent me over the years. Each one touched me in a special way. She is the one who sensed Jesus' saying I was "His Golden Girl" as I was in the Refiner's fire with my trial of Lupus. It was such a gift and a tremendous encouragement at the time. We are kindred spirits, and I love her dearly.

Amy's daughter Rebecca (Becky), my niece, surprised me by painting "The Lie" after she heard me tell Amy that part of my story. It was the first painting completed, and she gave it to me for Christmas. It is a treasure to me. It gave me a stronger desire to have the other visions painted as well.

My other sisters, Jeannette and Karen, and brother Ben have supported and encouraged me to share this story. It's close to home for all of my family, and I appreciate how they have embraced it.

Prayer Teams
I asked a small group of friends if they would pray for me after the traumatic memories were triggered and as I went in for counseling. It seemed impossible to go in on my own without them. I felt paralyzed with fear. Knowing they were praying for me gave me strength and courage. Because they knew me well, they were faithful to carry me in prayer to the feet of Jesus for healing. David Gater, Amy Knight, Julie Johnson, Pat Kelly, Nancy Wilson and Cara Janusz, your prayers meant so much to me.

Years later as I began to put the paintings and writing together into a book, I became stuck. Again, God provided a small group to pray for me. Nicole Given, Melissa Tinsley and Brenda Hollenbach were moved to pray, and poetry began flowing out of me! I experienced a noticeable difference after that time of prayer. How I appreciate the support, love and prayers of this sweet group.

My Friends
In the early stages of my rough draft, I had some extremely helpful input from trusted friends who read my words. Brenda Hollenbach, Melissa Tinsley, Susan Mittan, Kimberly Booser, and Cindy Lear gave significant input on the parts of my story that needed more clarity, suggesting additions and editing tips. My first mentor and lifelong friend, Priscilla MacRae, gave me some final editing advise that was crucial, which motivated me to rewrite a couple of awkward paragraphs that now I am very grateful to have done. DeFord Davis has become a dear friend through this project. She has spent a huge amount of time reading it multiple times and giving me wonderful editing comments and supportive input. She's been one of my biggest advocates. I am so grateful for each of these friends for their influence in my life as well as for their suggestions on this project.

DeFord and Brenda are involved in organizations (Women at Risk, International and Samaritan Creations) that support victims of sex trafficking. My heart goes out to the victims, and I commend the organizations trying to rescue, support, and restore these terribly wounded people. How I long to place my book in every safe house—better yet, in every victim's hands—to give them hope for healing and wholeness through Jesus. Any proceeds this book may bring will go to this cause.

My Counselor
Dr. Gregory Hocott was my psychologist. He is the owner of the Family Counseling Center in Ann Arbor, Michigan. He honestly described to me what was needed for recovery. He did not sugarcoat or water anything down. He explained that I needed to go into the tormenting memories and cry out to Jesus for healing from that wounded place. As horrible as that sounded, he was right. He validated all the imagery that I experienced and explained its importance in the healing process. Each appointment was valuable. Those sessions brought more than recovery; they validated the deep inner healing to the point of overflow in desiring to share my experience and joy with others.

My Art Instructor
Christaphora Robeers was my art instructor from Crossroads Art Center in Richmond, Virginia. She is an international artist who has tremendous expertise and experience. I especially appreciate her tenderness with me. She was gentle in her critiques. Somehow she knew these paintings were extremely important to me. Painting these images became almost an additional form of therapy, further ingraining into my mind all that had taken place. Even though I didn't have the skill to paint the visions exactly as I had seen them in my head, it was close enough to help me remember the beauty of what I had seen and experienced. Now I have the paintings all hanging in order in a special room in my home—my healing room. It's a sacred place where I take people to share my story one-on-one when God opens an opportunity.

My Models and Photographers
Nicole Cochran, David Gater and Amy Knight were excellent models for me. As models, they helped me recreate some of the images I wanted to paint. Nicole was a diver and reminded me of my younger self. David made an excellent Jesus (even without a beard). Amy, of course, modelled herself in "Amy's Hug." Looking back, I wish I had used models for all of my paintings. I believe the paintings became much better when I took this new approach.

A good friend, Scott Combs, took pictures of all my paintings to preserve the images during our move from Virginia to Pennsylvania, in case they were damaged. The photographs also gave me the opportunity to place the images into a book.

Taylor Barker, not only photographed the picture on the back cover of the book, but also helped me create the image and lighting of "His Golden Girl" to paint. And Robyn Blumhorst, photographed and helped create the image and lighting for the painting, "Come to Me."

My Graphic Artist
Shevon Johnson, an extremely talented graphic designer and artist, came back into my life at just the right time. I love when God does this! We were both Young Life leaders in Arizona during our college days. I saw her website and wanted to talk to her about how to put some of my paintings on a website to make them available for prints down the road. After a short time, I realized she was the person I was looking for to put my book together. With her artistic touch, she put together such a beautiful presentation of my story. Her work exceeded all my expectations. She also gave valuable input on additions and editing. She encouraged me in prayer when I hit a rough spot and felt stuck. It's been a pleasure working with her. I was grateful to know that my story was in hands I could trust and respect.

My Editors
As I was searching for the right fit for an editor, a surprising opportunity arose to talk to an established author, Deborah Waterbury. After seeing some of my art work and reading parts of my story, she gave me some extremely valuable input. She highly recommended two editors, Shanna Gregor and Rena Fish. Rena has been especially helpful in the deeper fine tuning of this work. I am so grateful for all of her input, including writing the back cover of this book!

Denise's resources and teachings can be found at
www.Hope4HealingHearts.org

To book Denise for a speaking event, write to
Hope4HealingHearts@gmail.com

To purchase a print of any of Denise's paintings, go to **www.DeniseGaterArt.com**

References

[1] *Passion: Our Love Is Loud (Live audio CD).* Brentwood, TN: Sparrow Records/Atlanta, GA: sixstepsrecords.

[2] Hall, C. (March 28, 2002). "Sweep Me Away". On *Passion: Our Love is Loud (Live* audio CD). Brentwood, TN: Sparrow Records/Atlanta, GA: sixstepsrecords.

[3] Olsen, Greg K. *Be Not Afraid*, 1997. Oil on canvas. www.gregolsen.com/gallery/be-not-afraid#optioncontent, accessed 9 Mar. 2016.

[4] Hurnard, Hannah. (1975). *Hinds' Feet on High Places.* Carol Stream, Illinois: Tyndale Publishers, Incorporated.

[5] Hall, C. (March 28, 2002). "Prepare the Way". On *Passion: Our Love Is Loud (Live) [audio CD].* Brentwood, TN: Sparrow Records/Atlanta, GA: sixstepsrecords.

[6] Lewis, C.S. (1950). *The Lion, the Witch and the Wardrobe.* New York, NY: Harper Collins Publishers.

[7] Wyatt, Will. (2005). *Discovery: God's Answers to Our Deepest Questions*, Revised Edition. Colorado Springs, CO. Dawson Media.

[8] Eldredge, John. (2009). *The Four Streams: How Christ Heals Our Hearts.* Colorado Springs, CO: Ransomed Heart Ministries.

[9] Edwards, M. (May 18, 2012). "Fling Wide". On *Once Dead Now Alive in Christ [audio CD].* Kansas City, MO: Forerunner Music.

"*Come to me, all you who are weary and burdened, and I will give you rest. Take my yoke upon you and learn from me, for I am gentle and humble in heart, and you will find rest for your souls. For my yoke is easy and my burden is light"* (Mathew 11:28-30).

Made in the USA
Middletown, DE
12 June 2023